YOUR MONEY
&
THE CASINO

WHAT TO KNOW BEFORE YOU GO

To David, All the best, in + out of the casinos! MO Rick

Missouri Rick

4-deuce Books, LLC

Hannibal, MO

Copyright © 2013 by "Missouri Rick" Schulten. All rights reserved.

No part of this book may be reproduced, scanned or distributed in any printed or electronic form without the express written permission of the publisher and/or the author.

Limit of Liability/Disclaimer of Warranty: While the publisher and author have used their best efforts in preparing this book, they make no representations or warranties with respect to the accuracy or completeness of the contents of this book and specifically disclaim any implied warranties of fitness for any particular purpose. The advice and strategies contained herein may not be suitable for your situation. You should consult with a professional where appropriate, either in taxes or otherwise. Neither the publisher nor the author shall be liable for any loss of profit or any other losses, including but not limited to special, incidental, or consequential damages.

Your Money & The Casino: What to know before you go.

ISBN: 978-0-9889717-0-7

Library of Congress Control Number: 2013933312

Published by: 4-deuce Books, Hannibal, MO

Editing by: With Pen In Hand, Atlanta, GA

Proofing: ERS Proofreading, Jersey City, NJ

Cover design by: ebooklaunch.com

10 9 8 7 6 5 4

DEDICATED TO THE LOVE OF MY LIFE

Debbie

YOU ARE MY GREATEST WIN EVER

AND TO OUR CHILDREN

Erin, Rusty & Erika, Adrienne

FOR MAKING PARENTING LOOK SO EASY

AND FOR MAKING US SO PROUD

SPECIAL THANKS TO

Frank & Dom

FOR SHOWING ME WHAT IT LOOKS

LIKE TO BE A WINNER

AND TO ALL OF THE

GTC crew

YOU KNOW WHO YOU ARE

Missouri Rick

TABLE of CONTENTS

	Introduction	1
Chapter 1:	Odds, Probabilities & Birthdays	5
Chapter 2:	The House Advantage	13
Chapter 3:	Bankroll Size & Casino Credit	21
Chapter 4:	On Tipping	35
Chapter 5:	Your Safety In The Casino	51
Chapter 6:	Getting Comps	57
Chapter 7:	Tips On Different Games	65
Chapter 8:	Paying Taxes	85
Chapter 9:	When Gambling Becomes A Problem	91
Chapter 10:	In The End, The Hold Is What Matters	95
Chapter 11:	Glossary, Or What It All Means	103
Chapter 12:	Bibliography	171

All The Best –
In And Out Of The Casinos.

Missouri Rick

INTRODUCTION

"Winning is the most fun!" Dominator, Golden Touch Craps

"Luck comes and goes, but knowledge is forever." Bill Burton, Gaming expert for About.com

"Do you want to go to the casino?" is my favorite question. Well, maybe my second favorite question, right after "Do you want to get something to eat?" Thankfully, many of the casinos today have great restaurants in them, so I can satisfy two desires in one location.

This book is not about where to eat at the casinos, but about winning when you get there – because *you know how to win*. Knowing how to win doesn't just happen; you have to learn what causes you to lose and how the casino really gets your money.

But first a little background on how I learned to become a winning player, because I did lose at first, just like everyone does in the beginning.

Several years ago, a new riverboat casino opened near my home in Missouri. Like everyone else, I went to see what all the excitement was about. Right away, I found out the river was not exactly "under the boat." In fact, it was on the other side of the highway, past some camp sites and trailers, but you could definitely see the river from the "riverboat." So the very first thing I learned was that *maybe* the casinos were a little sneaky.

I didn't play any of the games on my first few trips to the new casino. All of my friends were playing, as was most of my family. I knew that I too would soon be playing, but I didn't see any reason to learn how to play those games with my hard-earned money on the table.

Instead, I went to the book store and found a few books about Blackjack, and then I found about 10 more over the next few months. Next I bought all of the books about Craps – way more than 10! Amazon and I became very well acquainted, and I was lucky enough to become good friends with more than a few of the authors along the way. And then, somewhere along this journey I became known as Missouri Rick.

I didn't realize it at the time, but I was already on my way to becoming a winning advantage player. People ask me if I like to gamble, and I always say no, I hate to gamble, but I love to go to the casinos and play! Then I try to explain the difference between being a "gambler" and being an "advantage" player, usually into blank stares. To me, gambling is the same as losing, and I don't like losing.

An advantage player is someone who is very knowledgeable about the different casino games and the different bets and only plays those where there is a good chance of winning. An advantage player also knows the good bets and the sucker bets and only makes the very best of the good bets. The casino has to *win* your money from you; it is not just mindlessly handed over to them.

On occasion some people will win at the casinos based on pure luck and chance, which is gambling. Others will win (and win more often) based on playing the best games in the best possible way, thereby dramatically tilting the odds into their favor, which is the beginning of advantage play.

This book will explain that difference to you, and hopefully help you decide to become more of an advantage player and less of a gambler. No matter where you are in your casino experience though, this book will show you a few things that will make your next trip to the casino a little more enjoyable and a little more profitable as well.

Understanding how the casinos earn their money (by taking your money) is fundamental to understanding the relationship between your bankroll and the casinos' goals. If you can look at your wins and losses in the same way the casinos do, then you are on your way to knowing what games to play and how to play them in order to allow your money to last as long as possible. And you'll give yourself a decent chance of leaving the casino as a winner. Because as my friend Dom says in the quote above, "Winning is the most fun!"

Throughout this book, I will make many references and recommendations to my favorite authors and their specialty books, as well as to some great websites for you to view. Also included in the back of this book is an extensive glossary of over 550 gambling terms.

Some chapters start out with basic, general information and then progress deeper in material and detail, maybe even to the point of being overwhelming for the casual player. Only read as far as you need to in those chapters, the rest will still be there when you're ready for it.

So whether you are just beginning to learn what the casinos have to offer, or if you are a long time player (or somewhere in between) there should be something here for you. As Bill Burton says, "Luck comes and goes, but knowledge is forever."

One final thought before we get started. If you bought this book with the intent of throwing it in the bonfire at some big gambling protest and book burning – please go back to the store and buy all the rest of the copies off the shelf as well.

CHAPTER 1

Odds, Probabilities & Birthdays

"Never tell me the odds!" Harrison Ford as Hans Solo in *Star Wars*

"A successful gambler must understand the math and the odds behind the games." Kevin Blackwood in *Casino Gambling for Dummies*

"The 50-50-90 rule: anytime you have a 50-50 chance of getting something right, there's a 90% probability you will get it wrong." Andy Rooney, TV Commentator

What are the chances that I would start off with a chapter on odds and probabilities in a book on how these two things affect you and your money while in the casino? That's as close to a sure thing as you will ever find. The challenge is writing a chapter about math (that you will read) that doesn't sound like a chapter on math. (I have noted a few places where you can safely skip over a particular paragraph on figuring out the math if you like.)

The reason you need to have more than a passing knowledge of how odds work is so you can understand how big a risk you are taking and how bad the house advantage is going to be against you. These two things – the odds and the house advantage – are what make up gambling and drive how fast your money disappears into the hands of the casino.

Winning at gambling is all about making the bets that are the most likely to win, and avoiding the bets that give the house too much of an advantage. Therefore, in order to give yourself the greatest chance of winning, or at least not losing as much or as fast, you need to play the games with the best odds and with the lowest house advantage working against you.

Let's get started with a few definitions – such as "odds." "What are the odds?" is an expression everyone has heard and probably even used. The odds express how many times something *will not* happen in relation to how many times it *will* happen.

So what are the odds that today is Friday? The odds of today being Friday are 6 to 1 because there are six chances that today is not Friday, and one chance that today is Friday. (So is today Friday as you are reading this? The odds are against it.) Later in this chapter, we will discuss some other ways the word "odds" is used.

Now let's talk probabilities, as in what is the probability that today is Friday? Probability is the way of expressing a belief that a particular event *will* happen in relation to the number of ways it *can* happen. The probability that today is Friday is 1 in 7 because there is one chance that today is Friday out of seven total possibilities. See, that wasn't so hard after all.

Probability comes from the Latin word *probabilis* which means "resembling truth." Because the word means that it only resembles the truth, normal people who are not math wizards tend to treat the information inferred by probabilities in one of two ways: they either give it way too much importance (thinking that the event *will* happen), or they discount it tremendously (thinking that the event *can't* happen). Both decisions may cause the casual player to make extremely wrong and costly decisions at the tables. Often the 4:1 favorite will lose, and that is why it is called gambling.

Chance is another word for probability and is sometimes used instead. When we ask, "What are the chances?" we are really asking what is the probability that an event will happen.

Now let's try out some easy gambling examples of odds and probabilities. What are the odds that the first card dealt from the deck will be the Ace of Hearts? The answer is 51 to 1, also written as 51:1 or 51/1 because there are 51 other cards that it could be, in relation to the one card that is the Ace of Hearts. And what is the probability of that first card being the Ace of Hearts? It is 1 in 52, again also written as 1:52 or 1/52 because there is one chance that it is the Ace of Hearts, out of 52 cards. The probability of getting *any* ace is 4:52 or reduced to 1:13.

Let's do it one more time, only this time with a die (one is called a die, while two or more are called dice). What are the odds that we will roll a four? The odds are 5 to 1, because there are five ways not to roll a four and one way to roll a four. Everyone remembers that there are six sides on a normal die, right? Okay, now what is the probability that we will roll a four? The probability (or chance) is 1 in 6, as there is only one correct outcome of the six possible numbers or outcomes.

What about a coin toss? What are the odds of heads being the side shown? We will use only two choices – heads or tails, discounting the coin landing on edge or not coming down after you toss it into the air, both of which should be extremely rare occurrences. The odds of landing on heads will be 1:1 because there is one outcome that is not heads and one outcome that is heads. The probability of heads is one chance in two, or 1:2. (Try to remember never to play "Heads I win – tails you lose", or at least don't bet on the outcome.)

Finally, let's do a couple of roulette examples. What are the odds of the ball landing on a particular number, such as 22? Assuming we are playing on an 'American' wheel with the 0 & 00, then there are 38 pockets for the ball to land in. So the odds of hitting 22 are 37:1, while the probability (or chance) that we will hit the 22 is 1:38.

What about landing on Red or Black in roulette? Of the 38 numbers, 18 are Red and 18 are Black, with the 0 and 00 usually being Green (or some other color that is not Red or Black). The odds of hitting Red, therefore, are 20 ways not to land on Red and 18 ways to land on Red, for 20:18. The probabilities of landing on Red are 18 ways to land on Red out of 38 possibilities, for 18:38.

This is a good place to talk about "true odds" and the "payout odds," sometimes called "house odds." When in the casino, the odds that are mentioned have to do with the payout (or payoff) odds on winning wagers, which are less than the true odds. These payout odds are what give the casino the "house advantage" or HA. In order to stay in business and make a profit, the casino plans on paying out slightly less on winning bets than they take in on losing bets, thereby creating a profit, and the two different odds.

The bigger the difference between the odds of winning and the odds that are paid out, the greater the casino's HA is against you.

For instance, in the roulette bet on Red that we just discussed, the payout odds are 1:1 or even money. You bet one chip on Red, and if it hits, you win one chip. The issue is that there are 18 ways to win the bet on Red and 20 ways to lose it (don't forget the 0 & 00). The casino will win your chip more often than it loses it or pays it out, creating the HA of 5.26%, and showing that the payout odds are different from the true odds of winning.

(You can safely skip this paragraph on the math if you want to.) The player's expected value, the amount you should win or lose over the long term (or EV) when making a bet, is figured like this: (All of the ways to win) plus (all of the ways to lose) expressed as $(18/38 \times 1)$ plus $(20/38 \times -1) = 18/38 - 20/38 = -2/38 = -5.26$, which means that for every \$100 you wager, your expected loss is \$5.26. While it would be unusual for the casino to win exactly \$5.26, this figure is the average long term casino profit from each \$100 wagered on this roulette bet.

What this statistic really means is that no matter how lucky you are in the short term, the longer you play the more likely it is that the casino will win 5.26% of your money – in fact, the casino is counting on it! It is very hard for a player to overcome this high HA in the long term.

This HA is not a bad thing; you just have to know that it varies significantly from game to game, and even from bet to bet within a game. By arming yourself with the knowledge that certain bets have a very high HA, while others have a relativity small HA, you can (and should) "shop around" while you play, looking for and playing the lowest HA games and bets. This "shopping around" will give you the greatest chance of winning or at least a better chance of lasting longer and losing slower. The HA is covered in detail in the next chapter where I will show you what you need to know in order to protect your money.

You may have heard the expression "don't buck the odds." The casino is definitely not the place to buck the odds – if you expect to have any chance of winning consistently. Sometimes you will beat the odds and win, but usually you will lose your bets a little more often than you win them. Thankfully, at least the drinks are free!

So far, we've talked about true odds and payout odds which are important, but what about the third way to use the word odds, called the "odds bet"? Sometimes in craps, additional money is added to a bet and is called "odds," as in "Do you want to add odds to it?" This new combined wager has a mixed payout of payout odds on the first part of the bet, and true odds payout on the new money (the odds bet, or the second part of the bet), and it helps to reduce (or dilute) the HA against the player, although it does not change the overall odds of winning the bet. If this entire paragraph sounds confusing, you must not be a craps player. Don't worry; later in a chapter on games, we will discuss it in more detail.

Many games in the casino have odds that are not subject to change, such as craps, slots, roulette, and keno. However, there are a few games where the skill of the player may slightly alter the odds in his favor, such as blackjack, pai gow, and video poker. Just remember that even with the slightly altered odds, the HA will almost always still favor the house in the long run.

Another thing to be aware of is the way the payout odds are stated by the casino. Sometimes it is "something *to* 1," while other times it is "something *for* 1." For instance, in craps, the payout for a winning Hard 6 or Hard 8 bet at one casino is 7 to 1, and then in another casino it is 8 for 1. Which sounds better? Wouldn't you rather win eight chips instead of only seven chips? But the 7 to 1 is in addition to your chip, while the 8 for 1 includes your chip. In other words, the payout is exactly the same, but the sneaky casino tries to make one sound better than the other, in an attempt to lure your business.

Now let's have some fun and see where the odds and probabilities of birthdays may not be as intuitive as we would think. In a random group of 50 people, what are the chances that any two of them will have the same birthday? Not very likely is the common response, with only 50 people in the group and the thought that there are 366 possible birthdays in a year (Feb 29 is also a birthday). Everyone says that two common birthdays out of 50 people, given 366 choices is not very likely – in fact they will bet on it! Quickly working out the chances in your head seems to be 50 out of 366, which reduces to about 1 in 7.3 or so.

This birthday bet is a very famous problem in math classes that deal with probabilities, and there are really just two possible outcomes: either everyone in the group has a different birthday, or at least two people in the group share a common birthday.

To work it out, we will first determine the probability that each of the 50 people will have a different birthday. Then, from that answer, we can quickly see what the chances become that two will have the same birthday.

To find the first answer, we do the following multiplication problem: (you don't really have to do this at home!)

$365/366 \times 364/366 \times 363/366 \times \ldots \times 319/366 \times 318/366 \times 317/366 = 0.03$ or 3%

With a 3% chance they all have different birthdays we're left with a 97% chance that at least two share the same birthday in a group of 50 people! So therefore, those who bet on it, thinking it was only 1 chance in 7.3 (about 15% probable), usually will lose that bet.

(If you want to figure this at home remember the first person in the group has a birthday on some day, and this day is represented as 366/366 or 1. So the equation is 1 times 49 more choices for different birthdays, with a second person being a different birthday than the first shown as 365/366 (because one day is already used), and the next, which is different than the first and the second, will be 364/366 because two days are now used, and so on a total of 49 times. Be sure to relook at the math equation of this shown above.)

It turns out that 23 people in the room will become the breakeven point, with around a 51% likelihood that two or more will share the same happy day. Here is a table with the chances of sharing a birthday with different total numbers of people listed:

10 is 12%
20 is 41%
23 is 51%
30 is 71%
40 is 89%
50 is 97%
60 is 99%
70 is 99.9%
80 is 99.99%

The point is to show that all bets are not what they seem. The casino will advertise and display the bets that have the largest HA for them, but which are usually the worst bets for the player. When you hear a dealer offering you a bet or reminding you to make a bet someplace, look to see if it is a high HA bet; it probably is. They will advertise the bad bets often and loudly, and they are remarkably quiet about the good bets.

Your best bet to win, or least stay to play a little longer, is to understand the odds and probabilities, as well as how the HA is determined. Then find and play only the best games and the best bets in those games, those which have the lowest HA working against you and your money.

These games (very few) and bets (even fewer!) will be covered in Chapter 7.

CHAPTER 2

The House Advantage

"You lose when you lose, but you also lose when you win." Frank Scoblete, America's #1 Gaming Writer

"Casinos provide adult entertainment, and the House Advantage is the price of admission." Anthony Curtis, publisher of *The Las Vegas Advisor*

"If you want 21% in your advantage, pay off your credit cards." Andrew Tobias, Financial Advisor

    Casinos love winners. They will take your picture, bells and whistles will go off, and lights will flash. Everyone in the immediate vicinity will know someone is winning. The casino might even use your picture in an advertising campaign, with your permission, of course!

    Yes, all casinos love winners, and they really do want you to win.

    Many people believe that the casinos do not want you to win, and really nothing could be further from the truth. Without winners, people would soon stop coming, and the casinos would not have a shot at getting their money. Woe is the poor casino when the word gets out that it is impossible to win there.

Who wants to play at a casino where no one ever wins? Not me. I want to play at the casino where lots of people win, and win all of the time.

The casinos have to make money to pay the bills, and as a business, they must turn a profit. In order to stay in business, they must take in more money than they pay out. A saying commonly heard in Las Vegas is "This town wasn't built on winners."

In general terms there must be more losers than there are winners, and the casino accomplishes this in many different ways, but the one way they absolutely depend on is the 'house advantage'.

The house advantage, or from now on the HA, is the edge that the casino will win (on average) on each and every bet over time. This figure is usually expressed as a percentage of the player's bet or wager, such as 1.41% or 5.26% or 11.11%. It can also be called the casino advantage or edge. Sometimes, it is loosely referred to as the VIG, short for Vigorish. The VIG, however, is more correctly defined as a small fee added to a bet when the payout does not contain a built in HA.

Different games, as well as different bets within those games, all have a different HA built into them. There is one bet on the craps table that has a HA of 0.0%, which is the very best you could hope for, but it can usually be made only in conjunction with another bet that does have a positive HA expectation for the house. At the other end of the range there are certain terrible Keno bets where the HA runs in excess of 25%.

One of the purposely confusing tactics of the casino is to have seemingly countless different HA percentages on a multitude of different wagers. Some games are good and offer a reasonable chance of winning, and some games are so bad that you should just stay home and mail a check to the casino. At least you will have saved the gas money.

Wikipedia provides the following information about the HA: "Casino games generally provide a predictable long-term advantage to the casino, or "house", while offering the player the possibility of a large short-term payout. Some casino games have a skill element, where the player makes decisions; such games are called 'random with a tactical element.' While it is possible through skillful play to minimize the house advantage, it is extremely rare that a player has sufficient skill to completely eliminate his inherent long-term disadvantage (the HA) in a casino game."

As an astute player looking to have an above average chance of winning, your job in the casino is to search out the best games and the best bets within those games. By keeping the HA as low as possible, and with some luck thrown in, you will give yourself the greatest chance of overcoming the casino and the HA, and thus a chance of going home a winner as well.

You should know, however, that while the HA is not a theoretical number, it is an average over time. In the short run of only a few plays or only a few hours or days, you might be way ahead or breaking even or you might be way behind. But over a month of continuous 24/7 play, many hundreds of thousands of decisions will be made on all of these individual bets. Over this longer term, the HA will be very predictable and very, very close to the theoretical projection of the casino's expected win because of the Law of Large Numbers.

According to the Law of Large Numbers, the average of the results obtained from a large number of trials should be very close to the expected value and will tend to become even closer as more trials are performed. This law is important to the casino because it guarantees a predictable estimation of the hold, or wins over the long term. There are other ways that the casinos use to increase the hold, and these are covered in detail in Chapter 10.

The house has two more major advantages over the player: the size of the casino bankroll and the ability to keep the games going 24/7. We will discuss the individual bankroll and bet size of the player in another chapter, but for now, let's just say that the casino's bankroll is large enough to weather any short term swings in player winnings. Most of the time those winnings have close to no impact on the casino's ability to keep playing.

The main thing that the casino wants, indeed even needs, is the exposure of your bankroll to the HA over a period of time. The casino bosses want to keep you playing for as long as possible. They keep the doors open and the lights turned on around the clock. They will give you a room to spend the night if it means you will stay another day and continue to play. They will give you a comp'd meal if it means you will come back later and keep playing. They will give you a player's card to encourage you to keep betting a portion of your bankroll at one of the affiliated casino properties.

The casino management wants you to have a good time and to win, but they really do not care if you are ahead or behind right now, as the short term means nothing to the casino. They do not care if you just won a $6 bet or a $6,000 bet, or if you just lost that same amount.

What they do care about is that over a period of the last 30 days a total of $60,000,000 was wagered in their casino, and the overall HA of 10% was applied to that 60 million, for a gross profit of $6,000,000 to them. That is what the casino bosses really care about.

Based on the amount of the money that is wagered on all the different games over a given period of time, the HA will allow for a very close prediction of the actual projected profit to the casinos.

There are two main ways for the casinos to adjust the HA: they can adjust the payoff, or they can adjust the odds of winning. (There is also a third way, which is by adding a small fee (the Vig) to certain bets to create a HA where there was none before, as is found in some baccarat or craps bets.)

One quick example of the casino adjusting the payoff can be found in the recent change in 21 (Blackjack) where the winning natural blackjack will now sometimes be paid at a rate of 6 to 5 instead of the long-held standard of 3 to 2. A $10 bet that usually pays $15 at 3:2 now only pays $12 at 6:5, and the casino has an extra $3 drop through to the bottom line that they didn't pay out to the winner. That's a huge change to the HA, and it is definitely not in the players favor.

This book is not about how to play Blackjack, but just as a matter of principle I would never sit down to play at a 6:5 table, and you shouldn't either.

An example of changing the odds of winning, and thus changing the HA, can be found in roulette. On an 'American' wheel, you will find 36 numbers and two house numbers – the 0 and the 00 – for a total of 38 possibilities, with a HA of 5.26%. On the 'European' wheel, there is only a single 0, for a total of 37 possibilities, and a HA of only 2.63%. By simply adding one more space for the ball to land in (the 00), the odds of winning changed from 36:1 to 37:1, and the HA doubled!

Again, this is not a book on how to play roulette, but if everything else is equal, always try to play on a single 0 wheel, if you're lucky enough to find one.

And once again, understanding how the casinos earn their money (by taking your money) is fundamental to understanding the relationship between your bankroll and the casinos' goals. If you can look at your wins and losses in the same way the casinos do, then you are on your way to knowing what games to play and how to play them in order to allow your bankroll to last as long as possible.

The HA is really your projected loss (expected value or EV) when you make a wager. When we talk about 1.41%, this really means that for every $100 you bet, you will lose $1.41 on average, over time. Of course if you lose the bet, you will lose 100% of it. But when you win the bet, the casino becomes your silent partner, keeping a small portion (1.41% or $1.41) of your winnings as the HA. This retained portion of your winnings is the "price of admission" mentioned at the beginning of the chapter in the quote by Anthony Curtis.

Let me give you a few of the simpler examples to explain how the HA is figured and extracted. In craps, a 'place bet' on the 6 or 8 for $6 will pay $7 if won, but the true odds payout (based on the true odds of winning this bet) should be $7.20, not $7 even. In order to keep the payout simple and in order to create the HA, the casinos keep the 20 cents for themselves. This slightly less than true odds payout gives this wager a HA of 1.52%. After all, you just won $7, so what is an extra 20 cents? That small amount collected on each and every bet is the HA, and that is what keeps the lights on in the casinos.

So what a HA of 1.52% really means is that for every $100 you wager on a particular bet, you can expect to lose $1.52 (again – on average, over time), and the casinos plan on winning that same amount. And I will say it again – they count on it.

Okay, look the other way or skip the next two paragraphs if you don't want to see how the figures of $7.20 and 1.52% were arrived at.

In craps, there are six ways to roll a 7, and five ways to roll a 6 or 8. With a wager on either the 6 or the 8 there will be six ways to lose it and five ways to win it, making your odds of winning 6 to 5 against. The true odds payout on a $6 wager should be $6 times the chance of losing it ($6 x 6 = $36) divided by the chance of winning it ($6 x 6/5 or $36/5 = $7.20) for the true payout of $7.20, but as you know, the actual payout for the player is $7, with the extra 20 cents going to the casino.

Here is how the HA of 1.52% (or a -1.52% EV) is determined. Wagering $6 on the 6 or 8 a total of eleven times (six ways to lose and five ways to win) places $66 of your money at risk ($6 x 11 = $66). You expect to win five times to recover $65 (5 x $7 payout = $35, plus you get back the five wagers you placed of $6 for an additional $30). You have wagered $66 and you get back $65, so your expected value of that bet (series) is -$1. In order to arrive at the HA, we divide the expected value by the wager, or -$1/$66 for -0.01515. Now to get a percentage, we multiply by 100 to get -1.515%, and round up to -1.52%. Simple, huh?

Another easy example is found in roulette. With 38 spaces for the ball to land in (on a 0, 00 wheel), you have 37 ways to lose and one way to win. Your odds of winning a single number bet are 37:1, but the winning $1 wager is paid at the rate of 35:1, or $35, and not the $37 that the true odds would suggest. Guess who kept the other $2, thereby creating a HA of 5.26%. Hopefully by now you know it was your silent partner – the casino.

Okay, here is the math (this one is easier). When you bet $1 on 38 spins of the wheel, you should (on average) win $35 (the one win) and lose $37 (the 37 losses), which gives a net loss of $2 on the series of 38 spins. The expected loss per play then becomes 2/38 of a dollar, or 5.26 cents. What this paragraph really means for you and your bankroll is that for every $100 you bet at roulette, over time you are expected to lose $5.26. Whether or not you can overcome this HA with luck is why it is called gambling.

Frank Scoblete's quote, "You lose when you lose, but you also lose when you win" now begins to make a little more sense as you understand that the casino becomes your silent partner on every winning bet, extracting the HA to pay the bills.

You have agreed to pay the HA as the price of admission in order to play, so by playing games that keep that HA as low as possible, and with a little luck, maybe you can overcome the casino in the short term and go home a winner.

CHAPTER 3

Bankroll Size & Credit Play

"Don't lose money!" Warren Buffett's first rule of investing

"Money won is twice as sweet as money earned!" Paul Newman, as Fast Eddie Felson in *The Color of Money*

"Never play with money you cannot afford to lose!" Every gambling author in print

"How much money should I take, and how much should I bet?" These are the two main questions when it comes to the size of a player's bankroll.

Then comes, "How can I make my money last?" and "Should I open a line of credit at the casino?" While these answers may be different for everybody, I will attempt to make some generalizations here.

I definitely think you need dedicated money set aside for the sole purpose of gambling. In other words never use money to bet with that is intended for other purposes, such as paying the rent or buying the groceries. Budgeting for and building a gambling bankroll is the first step towards being a responsible gambler.

Your bankroll can be in the form of a savings account at the bank, or as simple as a portion of your money you keep separate from the rest, maybe in an envelope or other container. It matters less how it is kept and more that it is completely separate and specifically dedicated for the sole purpose of gambling.

I like a savings account with a casino line of credit against it. This works particularly well if you go to your regular casino often, or to a particular chain – such as Harrah's, with many affiliated casinos across the United States. This method also works well with larger amounts of money, so you don't have to carry a lot of cash around.

With the savings account method, you can set up an automatic deposit from your paycheck for a set percentage or specific amount each pay period and develop a substantial savings account over time. Any wins, at least in the beginning, should also be deposited back into the account. The intent here is to accumulate a large enough amount in your gambling account that you will be comfortable wagering a *small* portion of it without fear of going bankrupt.

Another advantage of this method is that most financial advisors recommend you develop an emergency cash fund of several months' worth of living expenses in case some type of financial disaster should strike you or your family. If that becomes the case, you can stop gambling, and use your saved up bankroll as a backup to live on. Don't, however, go the other way, and gamble away your cash reserves!

There is nothing wrong with gambling responsibly; the issue occurs when you gamble with money that you should not be using. In Chapter 9 of this book, you will find a list of questions to ask yourself to see if you may be having a problem gambling. If you answer yes to one or more of them, then you should stop and ask yourself if you should be gambling in the casino or not, and get help if you need it.

One ethical test you might like to use is called the newspaper test. Think to yourself what would happen if you were in the headlines tomorrow, showing everyone what you are doing right now with your money in the casino. Do you want to read, "…gambled away the rent money and now the family is homeless!" or "… lost the baby's milk money at the casino!"

If you would not like to read those headlines, or there are other people in your life who you would not like to read them, then maybe you are not doing the right thing. It is your money (hopefully) to do with as you please, but gambling is a lot more fun when you can gladly share your exploits with others.

How large should your gambling account be? Well, it depends on many things, such as how often you go to a gaming destination and how big you bet. If you just go to a local casino once a month or so, and then only play $20 through the slots, you will require a much smaller bankroll than if you go to a resort destination many times a year to play for days on end.

The point is that it should be of sufficient size to allow you to be comfortable wagering the amount you do and not have to worry about running out of money. You want your 'Risk of Ruin' (losing your entire bankroll) to be as close to zero as possible.

I like to be extremely conservative in my bet size in relation to my bankroll, and I feel that a good place to be at is a 1000:1 ratio of bankroll to bet size. While that sounds like a lot (and it is), it gives you a good margin against losing everything when lady luck turns against you.

If you normally bet 25 cents at a time in the slots, then maybe a goal would be to develop a gambling bankroll of $250. Of course, this amount can grow over time, and then you can increase your bet size. For example, $1 bets would call for $1,000 in the bankroll account.

If you are a $5 blackjack player, then this 1000:1 ratio would call for $5,000 in your gambling account. When I say a $5 player should have $5,000 backing him up, it sounds like a lot of money, and it is. Again, you can start with less and work towards saving this amount; maybe 500:1 or even less can be a goal to have along the way.

I also advocate you taking 10% (or less) of your total bankroll to the casino on any single playing session, again to give you staying power when luck turns against you and the bets don't go your way. So with a $5,000 total bankroll in your savings account, you might only take $500 to play the individual session and only make individual bets of $5.

At these levels and amounts, your risk of ruin is almost non-existent (assuming you are playing low HA games), and your bankroll will allow you to enjoy continued play long into the future.

Few things are more demoralizing than losing your entire stake each time you go to the casino and always needing to rebuild your bankroll again from zero.

Mine is a very conservative schedule, and many other authors will recommend different (lesser) amounts, such as taking 200 times your individual betting amount for slots, and at least 40 times your bet for table games. Others will say if you're playing nickel slots, you should bring 200 times 5 cents which is $10 to play with, and if you're playing at a $5 blackjack table you should have 40 times your $5 bet, or $200. Again, I am more conservative in my recommendations.

I look at gambling as an enjoyable long-term endeavor, such as a hobby, and I want to have sufficient funds available. I think that if you're a $5 bettor, then you will be more comfortable playing when you have at least $5000 in the bank to back you up, and then never worrying about losing everything. Your risk of ruin is nearly zero.

Maybe you are comfortable making $10 bets with a total of $200 to play with. That is fine, as it is your money, but just know you stand a much higher chance of being wiped out at that level. If you can replace that money easily through disposable income without impacting your lifestyle, then it is your money to do with as you please.

However, if you are a $25 bettor, I hope you will not go into a casino with only $200. I know everyone has a different comfort level, but imagine the feeling of having $25,000 set aside in your gambling account to back up your play, and you only have 10% of it with you on an individual trip. Then those $25 bets would make sense if you want to play at that level.

You may not get there right away, but with long term dedication, you can. If you want to play at a higher level, set a goal to accumulate the amount needed in your bankroll to sustain that higher level of play.

Now I hear the cries of despair, saying, "Hey, I only go once in a while, and I only play a $20 bill." Okay, I get it. As long as that money is specifically dedicated for that purpose, and not stolen from another portion of your budget, such as food for the family, then okay. If you budget a specific amount of your income to buy lottery tickets and gamble with, then at least you are way ahead of all those who don't budget for gambling at all. That dedicated amount is still a bankroll, just not a very large one.

In Chapter 2, when I discussed the house advantage (HA) I mentioned that two main advantages the house has over the average gambler, beside the built in house edge on every bet, is the ability to stay open 24/7 and the size of the casino's bankroll.

The definition of "Gambler's Ruin" is the following – A gambler playing a negative expectation game with a limited bankroll will eventually go broke against an opponent with an unlimited bankroll.

What the gambler's ruin really says is that when you play in a casino with a small bankroll, you're going to lose your money. How fast you lose it is determined by how high the HA is you are playing against and the size of your bankroll.

By having a large enough bankroll to stay solvent through the losing sessions and by finding and playing only the lowest HA games, you can extend your playing time and enjoyment and may even win a little money. In Chapter 7 we will discuss which games and which bets give you a decent chance of winning.

Now let's talk about stop-loss limits. A stop-loss is setting a limit on how much you will allow yourself to lose when the bets are not going your way before you stop playing, so you don't lose your entire bankroll in one session.

Say that I am that $5 blackjack player, and I took $500 with me to the casino to play an individual session. I would buy in for the entire amount and plan on not losing more than half. If I got down to $250 left, I would stop the session and walk away. If you can't do that, then don't take the $500 in with you, take only $250. When the bets are not going your way, you should stop playing. Do not, instead, keep playing until your planned time at the casino is up or until all of your money is gone.

I never like to see anyone lose the entire amount of the buy in, and then have to leave completely busted. Losing everything you came with is poor bankroll management, and is extremely demoralizing. If luck is not going your way, then stop. I like to set a 50% loss limit, and if I hit it, I stop. You never know how long a losing streak will last, or a winning streak for that matter.

So what about when you are winning? Good for you, but now you need to protect that win. A rolling stop loss also adjusts your stopping point when you are winning. Say I am ahead $200. Now I would stop if I gave back one half of my winnings, or $100.

This rolling stop loss would guarantee me a win of at least $100. If I continue to win, then I continue to adjust my stop-loss upwards to preserve most of the win.

Some other writers advocate setting a win goal and stopping when you hit it. I have never agreed with this policy, and have discussed it with a lot of people. When you are winning, keep playing if time allows – just don't miss your bus! Just make sure to adjust your stop-loss upwards, and you'll keep increasing your winnings. If you double your money, then good for you! If you now have won ten times what you started with, great; you're buying dinner!

Don't stop your winning just because you get to some predetermined number or amount. Keep going, but remember to stop when the tide turns (it always does) and quit playing when you hit your newly adjusted stop-loss. Never give it all back to the casino.

When you are winning, avoid the attitude that you are now playing with the casino's money, because you're not! It is your money after you win it. Security would not let you leave if it were the casino's money. Don't change your style of play and become reckless because you're ahead. That new money is your money, and you should protect it just as you would if it were your original bankroll.

Most people get ahead at some point in their play, yet most also cash out at the end of the session with a loss because they will not stop playing until the allotted money or time is gone.

I understand this line of reasoning. What would you do if you drove or flew all the way to the big casino destination and then got lucky and won right off the bat? You came to play, and you don't want to stop right away. You win a bunch right away, and then slowly you start giving it back. I say you should stop playing, cash in, and go do something else for a while. Eat, sleep, sightsee, see a show, go to the pool or just walk around a bit, but keep the money you won from the casino – because now it is your money. Don't give it back.

If I win early, that just leaves me more time for the other things I enjoy. Imagine how much more enjoyable your trip will be when you know that you're already going to go home a winner! There are lots of fun things to do while at the casino, and I know the entertainment factor is huge, but the main reason to go is to win and then go home a winner.

Just in case you don't already know, I will remind you that casinos are not designed to give away money; you have to win it from them. And as Fast Eddie Felson (Paul Newman) said in *The Color of Money*, "Money won is twice as sweet as money earned!"

Gambling is considered to be adult entertainment, just like going to an amusement park or the races, or whatever else you like to do for fun. You budget a certain amount of money to spend at the park for entertainment, and you do the same thing when you go to the casino: you plan on losing a certain amount of money while you are there as the "cost of entertainment."

I do not plan on losing any money when I go to the casino to play. I have the limited ability (bankroll backing me up) to lose, and I do lose on occasion, but I never plan on it. When I am losing, I stop playing, and cut my losses short. Then I do something else, besides losing money, for entertainment. Sometimes I think I hate losing more than I like winning, which may be true.

Warren Buffett's first rule of investing is "Don't lose money!" Rule #2 is "Always remember Rule #1." I like to use these two rules when I am playing to help stay focused on the task at hand, which is winning, and then keeping the win.

The different shows, the different local sites, the different restaurants, the pools, friends – there is always something to do at a casino besides gambling. The casinos want you to gamble the entire time you are there. They would like you to play for 24 hours a day if it were possible. They want and need exposure to your bankroll for as long as possible in order to apply the HA against it. (See Chapter 2 for a refresher on the HA.) Your first job in the casino is to protect your bankroll; your second is to have fun and win.

Now a bit about playing sessions. Your gambling play is divided into short sessions of up to several hours at a time. (Read in detail about sessions in Chapter 8 on taxes.) A single evening trip of a few hours would be a session. If you go for the weekend, you might have a Friday night session, three sessions on Saturday, and two sessions on Sunday, for a total of six individual sessions for the trip.

So if you take $3,000 with you on this trip to gamble with, you should break that total up into six individual $500 session bankrolls. Do not play with the entire $3,000 in the first session. If you lose the first $500, then you stop, and you do not get the next $500 until the next session. Hopefully, if a session is going against you, you will stop if you have lost half. Then if you lose all six sessions (it could easily happen!), you still go home with $1,500, which is far better than returning home broke! If you have a win on a session, adjust your stop-loss upwards for that session only and still begin the next session with the allocated $500.

Imagine a scenario where you are standing in a long line to check into the casino hotel, and you say to your spouse that you will be right back while you stroll into the attached casino. How would it go for you if you came back in a few minutes and said, "Don't bother to check in; I just lost all of our money!" That would not be a very happy trip home, assuming you're even included on the trip home. Good bankroll discipline avoids situations like this one and helps to make most of your playing sessions enjoyable.

Good bankroll management is a skill that is usually learned through trial and error. The smart thing to do is learn from other people's trials and errors when you can.

One other thing you may want to consider, after you have gained some experience and have built up a playing bankroll, is to open a line of credit at the casino.

Larger casinos offer a credit line to players to make betting your money more convenient. After establishing a credit account, you are basically signing a check that can be deposited into your bank should the need arise. You then ask for a "marker" at the table for the amount you are requesting. The dealer will call over a floor person or a supervisor in the pit area who will take your player's card and ID and print out the paperwork slip for you to sign, then the dealer will give you the correct amount of chips.

If you want a marker for playing slots, you usually need to make this request at the cashier's cage, although sometimes a slot attendant can do it.

To set up a credit account, go online to the casino's website and fill out the credit application. Or you can visit the cage at the casino to fill one out, but know it may take a day of two for the approval to come through.

When you are finished playing, you go to the cashier's cage to settle up your account, and know that there may be a separate room or desk to go to instead. If you have won, you pay off the marker, and keep the difference, which is sometimes referred to as "the white meat". If you have lost, you are expected to pay off the marker in a predetermined amount of time, which can be anywhere from that day to several weeks, usually depending on the amount of the marker. Check your individual casino for those details.

Signing a marker is just like signing a personal check from your bank so keep that in mind when you are using casino credit and do not sign for money you do not have or cannot afford to lose.

Also, a marker is not a free loan to use as you please. It is like legal tender in exchange for chips to use in that casino. If you take a marker and then leave with the money (known as walking with the money) without settling up at the cage, you will probably lose your credit privileges. Although this is not illegal, it is considered to be extremely bad form.

Casino credit provides a great customer service and makes playing in the casino quite convenient for you. Having a line of credit at three or four of the largest chains will allow you to play in most of the casinos in the US, as they are all becoming more and more affiliated.

Your safety is also improved because you do not have to carry large amounts of cash through the airport and parking garage or to and from your hotel room, and you will not have to cash checks, use the ATM, or take expensive credit card advances.

Having said that, getting easy money in the form of credit at the casino can be a terrible problem for those who cannot play within their budget, or for those who may have impulse control issues. No matter the convenience, you should never apply for a credit line if you do not have the discipline to control your gambling.

If you know that you do have impulse control issues, do not go to the casino with your credit card. Take in only what cash you can afford to lose. Few things are worse than losing your session stake of cash, draining your bank account with your ATM card, and then maxing out your credit cards with cash advances.

Never borrow money from friends or family in order to play. Losing the money will seem minor compared to the damage that you may do to your friendships and family. Borrowing from disreputable sources (loan sharks) brings an entirely new set of problems to your life and should never be considered.

The bottom line is never play with borrowed money. If you do not have the money, do not go to the casino!

Here is a good place to discuss 'scared' or 'sacred' money, which is any portion of your cash that you are afraid to lose or can't afford to lose, such as the grocery or rent money. Every gaming author since the beginning of books in print has said not to play with scared money, and I will repeat this warning again, "Never play with money you cannot afford to lose."

Playing with scared money (which is a poor decision) will likely cause you to make even poorer betting decisions because you will feel that you must win. You should know, however, that you cannot change the odds with poor betting decisions or poor bankroll management. Nothing good will come from playing with scared money, and you cannot ever win in this situation.

If you find yourself playing in such a way that you are no longer in control, please read the information in Chapter 9 on gambling problems and get help someplace. Gambling is supposed to be fun and enjoyable. When it isn't, please stop playing.

As a side note, if you know you have a gambling problem, you can voluntarily have your name placed on the exclusion list at the casinos, and then the casino security will refuse to allow you to enter or play. This may help you if you're unable to resist your urge to gamble when you have a problem.

One last thing is always have some form of photo ID with you when you are playing. You may need to show it in order to enter the establishment, and you may need it in order to cash out your winnings at the cage. You may need to show it at the desk to get a replacement room key or in a shop to use your credit card. Security might stop you somewhere along the way during a routine spot check. It is just a generally good practice to have it with you and especially when you are in a casino.

To recap: build a playing bankroll, set stop-losses, budget for session play, use casino credit wisely, never borrow to play, have your photo ID with you, plan on winning and have a good time. Remember that casino gaming is adult entertainment, and winning just makes it that much more fun.

CHAPTER 4

On Tipping

"I wonder if it isn't just cowardice instead of generosity that makes us give tips." Will Rogers

"When in doubt – tip." Missouri Rick

When we talk about your money and the casino, the question of tipping always comes up. Who, how, when, and how much are the usual things people want to know. Toking (tipping) the dealers and various service people can be an overwhelming experience to someone who is not used to being catered to every moment.

Gaming is a service industry, and many of the casino destinations are in service-based cities. Most of the people you interact with at the casino and hotel/resort will strive to provide you with good or great service with the hope that you will receive a good value for your money and then return again to spend more money with them.

Most, if not all, of the people with whom you directly interact with are low or minimum wage workers and depend on tips to supplement their income in order to make a living. Of course, tips are not required, but they are always suggested for good service, and good service means something different everywhere you go. Good service in Tunica, Mississippi, can drive a person from New York City crazy (but it is fun to watch – both the service and the crazy), while similar service in Las Vegas can totally bewilder someone from a rural background who is used to doing things for themselves.

Bellmen, skycaps, cab drivers, doormen, valets, concierges, check in desk clerks, room service personnel, maids, pool and spa attendants, waiters, servers, runners, change persons, slot attendants, and finally the dealers, everyone gets something, often over and over again. Just remember that while tipping is expected, it is in return for good service. You can always adjust the amount of your tip up or down, depending on the quality of the service provided.

Sometimes poor service happens, and you may be tempted not to tip, but I reserve that action for rude service, which I feel is different. Sometimes your meal is not right, or the extra towels didn't make it to the room on time, or whatever – poor service sometimes happens. I tend to think that people always try to do a good job, but they are occasionally overwhelmed by events as they try to do their job, thereby resulting in less than great service. As long as that poor service is not the consistent standard of the service provided, it's best to tip, even if it means a slightly smaller tip. At least, give them the benefit of the doubt the first time it happens.

Rude service, on the other hand should never be tolerated or tipped, and can be dealt with in many ways. Always make it a point to complain to management when you are treated rudely, as they will usually be glad to know about a small problem before it becomes a very big problem. Management at all levels in the casino usually has a very wide range of remedies to take care of any issues that arise with customer service. They want you to be happy so you will stay and continue to play there.

When playing in the casino, I never tip dealers for rude service, and I try to make sure the offending person knows why. On the game tables, tips are usually shared among dealers, so peer pressure works wonders. Tell the other dealers, specifically, why you are not tipping this particular time.

But you should also try to put yourself in the dealers' shoes for a moment and think about their days or shifts. They may stand there and deal to drunk, rude, obnoxious people all day. Some players are dirty and smelly. Some are mad or upset because they have lost everything. The dealers see tears, hear arguments, and often have profanity directed at them; they may even have cards thrown in their faces. They hear the same come-ons, complaints, and jokes all day long. They answer the same questions about how to play the hand and have to explain the rules over and over and over again. Their boss watches them like a hawk, thinking they will steal or make mistakes, and the players constantly think they are being cheated by the dealers. After a while, dealing the game becomes second nature, and the dealer can become bored out of his mind, fake a smile, and carry on a personal conversation with another dealer, all while dealing the game to you.

I am not making excuses for the dealers, just trying to put you into their frames of mind for a moment. Of course, not all dealers have shifts like I described, but some do. You breeze in from the pool on the way to a show or the steak house in your nice clothes, decide to play a bit, and wonder why the dealer isn't quite as chipper as he was earlier in the day. Now you know.

So I understand why rude service sometimes happens. After reading the last few paragraphs and thinking about it for a bit, I am surprised the dealers can even smile, let alone provide good or great service. I know I am not cut out for that position, so I always appreciate a pleasant, competent dealer.

Most dealers do a great job and are very proud of the service and professionalism they provide. It is always a pleasure to interact with the dealers who take pride in their skills and the services they deliver, and they should be tipped well. I will address tipping the dealers more in a bit, but first let's cover everyone else.

The first thing you will need to do is always make sure to have plenty of ones and fives available. It is very embarrassing to have empty pockets when someone has provided a service, and you have to tell them, "I will catch you later." Save your pocket change in a jar on your dresser and cash it in for one dollar bills before you go to the casino, as a one dollar bill is usually the minimum tip to offer.

Now a few general guidelines about tipping. Don't tip if it is not deserved (don't reward rude service). Tip discreetly. If you take up space at a restaurant table for an extra-long time, tip extra. Tip above the norm if you have been an extra burden, or if you are a regular. If the initial tip is larger than normal, it will pay benefits in the long run. If you use a coupon, tip on the full amount before the discount, and finally, when in doubt – tip.

Another general rule of thumb is when someone goes out of his or her way to provide a service that is over and above normal, then you should tip over and above normal. That being said, the following is a generally accepted guideline for tipping in different situations. It is a guide as to how I tip, which may be a little more than some people do, but it is what I am comfortable with.

The person who hales a cab and opens the door for you gets $1-2, unless he loads luggage or gets a big vehicle for a group. Then the tip is usually $1 per piece of luggage or per person, with the minimum then being $5.

If the cab driver is pleasant, speaks your language, and takes you straight to your destination, then he should be tipped a nominal amount (10-15%) on top of the fare, especially if he handles your luggage for you. I try to round it up to the next size bill and tell him to keep the change. So if the ride was $16, I will hand the driver a $20 which includes the tip (assuming this total amount also covers the extra luggage handling, otherwise you may need to pay a little more.)

If you use a limo service, then the standard tip to the driver is $20 (or $5 per person), especially if he does a good job and certainly if he helps with any luggage. Remember, if the limo ride was provided for free, the driver still gets a tip.

The shuttle bus driver at the airport receives $1-2 for the ride, especially if he helps with your luggage. For a couple with a bag apiece, $2-5 is fine. If the weather is terrible, and the driver picks you up from or delivers you directly to your car, then maybe $5-10.

If you drive yourself to the casino, always try to use the Valet parking instead of the self-park areas. Your safety is certainly always an issue, and while this isn't a book about the psychology of gambling, using the Valet parking will help put you in a "winners" frame of mind. As for tipping, remember that the person who takes your vehicle may not be the same person who retrieves it for you, so you will probably need to tip twice. When dropping off the car, $1-2 or a $5 to take your car is okay (more if you request special handling, like "keep it handy here by the door," something like a $20). Then I always tip at least $5 when the car is brought out to me. If you are driving a very high end car, a larger tip may keep you from appearing to be a cheapskate.

At the hotel, the bellman that unloads your bags and takes them inside for you should get $1-2 per bag, with a minimum of $5 for multiple bags. This amount is also the same for a Skycap at the airport.

The same goes for the person who later delivers the bags to your room. You haven't even unpacked yet, and you may have already tipped three or more people for handling your luggage. Another reason to pack light!

At the hotel check-in, the receptionist has a great deal of latitude in the type of the room you receive. A tip here goes a long way toward improving the quality of your stay. Be sure to mention if this is your first stay or your first trip to the city or if it is your honeymoon or anniversary. That information may get you a room upgrade for free and is certainly worth mentioning, but only if it is true. Otherwise you have to pay like the rest of us.

When you hand over your credit card, along with your player's card and ID, include a folded bill and discreetly ask if there are any room upgrades available. Think about this for a minute – a room with a view of the strip instead of the parking garage or a room looking over the lake, the ocean, or the golf course instead of the construction project next door. Or maybe a room at the end of the hall instead of the one next to the elevator. Or an 850 square foot room instead of a 550 square foot room or a mini suite with a hot tub instead of a standard room.

The person at the front desk checking you in will know all of this information and a lot more, so a tip here will go a long way. If you prefer a room nearer the elevator, just ask. Some people do for the safety of the extra foot traffic instead of an isolated room at the end of the hall.

So, how much you ask? Well it depends on a lot of things, like the location and time of year. If it is off season or midweek you may get by for a little less. The Bellagio will require more than the Flamingo. Vegas will require more than Tunica, and so on. The least I have used for this is $20, and the most is $50. Usually the desk clerk will return your money if he or she is not able to provide you with an upgrade, especially if you are pleasant and easy to deal with.

While this tip may sound like a lot up front, if you divide it out over the number of days you are staying, it can make for a very inexpensive and nice room upgrade. However, if you are demanding or rude, the clerk will usually keep the money, tell you that you received an upgrade, and then move you to the worst room available, which serves you right.

If the concierge arranges show tickets, a tour, or spa and hair appointments, then a tip of $5-20 is usually expected. If they work out something fantastic for you, then more (much more!) depending on the event and your budget. Nothing is expected when they only give directions.

Casino hosts are usually forbidden to accept cash tips, so small gifts are fine. Something like a tie, flowers, a chocolate tray – anything along these lines will be appreciated. Or a nice letter to the casino's general manager, telling how your host made this stay the best ever, would probably be appreciated more than anything.

The housekeepers and maids who clean your room daily have one of the least appreciated jobs at the hotel or resort, and they also have the ability to make your stay more pleasant, so you definitely want them on your side during your visit. There are several ways to tip these people, none of which are wrong. The main difference is whether you tip daily or one larger amount at the end of your stay.

I prefer to tip on a daily basis for several reasons. First, I want the housekeepers to know that they are going to be tipped right from the beginning, with the thought being that the service will start great and get better as you go along. If you wait until your departure to leave a tip in the room, you will only receive the normal minimal housekeeping services throughout your stay. My other concern about tipping upon departure is that I worry that one housekeeper will work all week in my room, and then if I happen to depart on her day off, someone else will pick up the tip. I try to meet with the housekeeper on the first day to determine the schedule and find out if the tips are shared or not.

Often if there is a person who comes around and strips the linen, they will pick up a tip left on the pillow. Then the housekeeper comes in and does all of the work of remaking the bed and cleaning the room, and receives nothing! (Unless tips are shared.) A few dollars on the pillow, as well as an envelope with $3-5 (or more) on the desk or TV each day will take care of this issue nicely. (And if your room is larger than your house, then kick it up a notch.) Always learn the hotel policy on this first, as some hotels will only allow money to be picked up as tips from the pillow top and no place else.

Room service should receive $1-2 for each item delivered, and more for something special, like bringing a refrigerator to the room.

Room service food delivery will usually already have a delivery charge tacked onto the bill, but it is still good form to tip the delivery person a few dollars for running it up to you. I do $2-5 for delivery to the door, and $10-20 for setting up the meal in the room, depending on complexity.

Now let's talk about dinner in the restaurant and how the tips should work there. Today, 15% is considered the normal tip, with a range of 10% for lesser service to a high of 20% for outstanding service. For those of you who don't keep a calculator handy, here is an easy way to figure it out: drop the last digit off of your bill and you have 10%! For example, if the total is $78.50, just drop the 0 from the end leaving you with $7.85, which is exactly 10%. Now for ease of figuring, round that amount up to the next whole dollar, or $8.00. Doubling that amount gives you $16.00, which is 20%, so your tip range for 10-20% is $8.00 to $16.00. On your $78.50 bill, if you leave a $100 for payment, you would be tipping $21.50, which is a little above the 20% end of the range (27.5%). $90 would be about 15%.

Always tip more if you are going to sit there forever. If the staff could have served another person in the extra time you took, then an extra tip is in order. You might also mention to the host or the waiter your intention to stay a little longer, as well as your plan to tip a little more, as this will help keep everyone's attitude in check.

Always look at the bill when it arrives to see if a tip has already been added in, as it is now somewhat customary with groups of six people or more. More and more, this added-in tip is beginning to show up on every bill, no matter how many seated at the table.

One scenario that I have seen many times is when the bill comes with the tip already added in, and then the person who is paying adds a second tip onto the credit card bill, and then another person throws a third tip out onto the table. Just be aware of this, and discuss it with the others at the table when appropriate.

Often, if I am picking up the tab for the meal, the other person will offer to leave the tip, which is fine. Just be sure to see if it is already included in the bill. If it is, maybe I get this one and he or she can buy next time.

On a meal that is comp'd by the casino, only the food and drinks are taken care of, and not the tip. When you have received a free meal, still remember to tip an appropriate amount for the service provided. The same goes for a discounted meal with a coupon; the service was still the same effort, and the tip should be figured accordingly.

If you're eating at a buffet, there may be a tip jar at the cash register to drop a few dollars into, but a tip here is not really required. However, if a person comes around to bring the drinks and refills to your table, then that person should be tipped $1-2.

The host who seats you should receive $2-5 for normal seating, or more if it's that type of a high-class joint, and even more if he or she fits you right in without a reservation or gets you the great seats, with $20 or more not being unusual.

At a show, the person showing you to your seats should receive $2-5, unless they get you a serious upgrade in the quality and location of your seats.

Look at your ticket stub to see if the seats are pre-assigned or not, and ask discretely if upgrading the seats is possible. Look at the posture of the person waiting to lead you in. Is he standing with one hand open at his side, the palm facing you? That is the glaring, universal sign that he is expecting a tip and that you can expect something in return. While $5 might get you your original seats or worse, a $20-100 bill might have you sitting in the front row or in that special spot where the entertainer comes out into the crowd. Trust me, after Barry Manilow has serenaded your wife, you will be glad you were not cheap this particular time! Good luck.

At the spa, beauty parlor, or barber shop 15-20% of the bill is considered normal for good service.

Washroom attendants usually receive nothing, unless you use the supplied toiletries, or they do provide some type of service. Then $1 is fine.

At the pool, the towel and drink people should get $1-2 each time they bring you something. If you want great service, try $5 the first time, and then $1-2 each time after that.

The same goes for the cocktail waitress in the casino: $1-2 for each round of drinks, and more if you're ordering for the group, at least $1 per drink, with a $5 minimum for a full tray. Hey – the drinks are free, so the least you can do is tip the waitress when they are brought to you. Even if you are only ordering water, still tip.

Here is a good place to say that tips can be paid with chips. The casino chips are the same as money to every employee in the casino hotel. I use chips to tip the casino waitress and dealers; everyone else gets folding money, but either way is completely acceptable.

Cigarette girls get $1-2 every time you purchase from them, and Keno runners get $1-2 every few rounds of play, or maybe $5 or so after the meal if you are playing while sitting and eating.

Change attendants who pay out winnings to slot players should receive something for their effort. If they have just counted out $1,199 into your hand, you will seem cheap to give them $5. While $5 is too little, I think $100 is too much, so maybe $20 is the right number here.

So now let's talk about tipping the dealers, as there are two schools of thought here, each of which has drawbacks. Some like to tip as they play (as I do), while others like to tip when they are finished playing. Again, either way is fine but let me go over the issues with both.

Tipping while you play shows that you are a tipper, and may help to facilitate better service during your playing time. By tipping at the end of play, you may be missing out on that "better" service that may have been available (but you will really never know about this). Tipping during play also prevents not having a tip available at the end when you have lost all of your session bankroll to the game – ouch.

Another advantage of tipping during play is that questionable calls and decisions are more likely to go your way. If there is a dispute on the table, the crew and the boss are more likely to decide in your favor when you are "taking care of the boys". Also the table rules might become slightly more favorable to a tipper, making for an overall better experience, but never count on this.

If you tip during play, a bet for the dealer every few hands is the way to do it, and I will cover how to do this in more detail in a bit. You can always ask the dealers where and how to place a bet for them; they will be very glad to show you.

Another big advantage to tipping while playing is that it puts the dealers into the game with you. If you win, they win. You won't have to worry about the dealers rooting against you when they have money on the line with you.

The down side to tipping while playing is that you are spending your session bankroll when you are tipping, thus having less money available to bet with. During a losing session, this tipping style brings the end that much faster.

A quick note, while tips are always appreciated, they are not really expected by the dealers when you are losing. I don't agree with this, as the dealer is still providing you the service – win or lose. Assuming it is an honest casino and game, it is not the dealer's fault that you are not winning.

The other way to tip is at the end of the session when you are coloring up (cashing in your chips – assuming you have chips left to cash in). If you have lost your buy in, you will have no chips left to color up, and thus no chips to tip with. Again – ouch.

If you do plan to tip at the end, make sure you save some chips for a tip. The dealer expects people to lose all of their money at the table, so showing that you're capable of using your last few chips for a tip, rather than for "one last chance" will be a pleasant surprise for a dealer. This tipping action can be beneficial if you play for long periods of time or will be seeing the same dealers every day. It can also help you build discipline with your bankroll; it takes a lot of control not to play with those last few chips, and instead give them to the dealer as a tip.

And as said earlier, tipping at the end of your session leaves you more chips to bet with during your session because you are not cutting into your bankroll for tips.

Let's say that it is the end of your session, and now you are going to color up (cash in your chips) $741 in chips, after buying in for $500 for a $241 win. Good for you, as winning is certainly better than losing, and a lot more fun. The dealer places in front of you a chip stack containing 1 purple chip ($500), 2 black chips ($200), 1 green chip ($25), 3 red chips ($15) and 1 white chip ($1) for a total of $741. While 10% of the $241 win is $24, you might leave the dealers the 1 green chip, 2 of the red chips, and the single white chip, or $36, which is a tip of around 15%. After going to the cage to convert the remaining 4 chips into cash, you have $705 left for a $200 profit (40%!) and $5 for the valet.

As a technical note, the IRS would consider the entire $241 as a win or income, not the $205 you're left with in this example because gratuities are not considered to be losses and cannot be counted against your win.

What if you only win $208 and have $708 to color up – now what? Only give the $3 or the $8? You can always ask for change from of one of the black chips if needed, but that is cumbersome. Or what if you have lost, and now have $341 to color up? Do you still feel like handing over $36 in tips? Or even worse, if you only have $41 (or nothing) left when you decide to stop playing.

I like to tip during play, and if it has been a winning session, I *also* tip when I color up. Trust me, if you are a regular at a particular casino, the dealers will remember your name. I'm always amazed when I return to a casino after being gone many months or more and the table dealers great me with a big "Mr. Rick – Welcome back!"

So how do I tip during play? I like to play craps, and I have nearly continuous bets up for the dealers while I am playing. I only make the best bets when playing, and I usually win those bets far more often than I lose them. By placing a chip for the dealers on top of my own bet, the dealers are in on the wins and get paid every time I do.

When playing blackjack, I make a dealer bet after every 10-15 winning hands or so, or about every 5 minutes, and again on top of my bet. Be careful here, don't tip so much or so frequently that you significantly shift the small edge you may have by giving away your wins.

In craps, when I have a pass line bet, I place a smaller denomination chip on top of my bet as a dealer bet, so when I win my bet I also get paid for the dealer bet on top. I then push the dealer's part of the win into the crew and leave the original chip on top of my next bet. I can win many bets and dealer bets this way, and I have only provided the original chip. So I may have pushed in to the dealer 2-10 chips or more as tips, but I provided only that *first* chip. Of course, when you lose that bet, the dealer chip goes away as well.

I always say that I control the bet, and several things happen. First, the dealers do not take it, as they know it is a bet for them and they know they only get the winning part of the bet (not the entire tip bet). Normally, the dealers are required by house rules to take the winning chip *and* the betting chip that provided the win. Second, if the dealer bet is on top of your bet, it will be counted towards your action by the pit crew for comp purposes, and you get double bang for your buck. If you put the bet beside your bet, or fail to say that you control it, the dealers will usually take that chip (plus any chips won) as a tip for them, and the pit may not count it towards the amount of your action.

Another bet I put on the table for the craps dealers are place bets. Usually I play with a group of friends, with two to five of us on each end of the table. We will often have one end of the table put out place bets for the crew on the 4-5-6, and the other end of the table put out place bets on the 8-9-10. (When I play by myself, I usually try to cover all of these points for $1 each; having a total of $6 on the table for the crew) This is between $1-10 (or more) on each number for the crew. We always say that we control these bets so they are not taken down when a number is rolled, staying up to win again and again.

Also remember not to hand tips directly to the dealer; they are not allowed to take money or chips from a player's hand. Place the tip on the table and push it part of the way forward and tell the dealer it's a tip by saying "dealer money." He will then pick it up and thank you.

Now a little about tip hustling. When the dealers ask for or demand a tip, it is considered toke hustling and is generally frowned upon or against the house rules in most US casinos. However, it is a widespread practice at casinos around the world, so be forewarned. That being said, I cannot tell you the number of times I play at a craps table with 12-16 people crammed around it, and I (or my friends and I) am the only person tipping the crew. At the beginning of this chapter, I said to tip discreetly, but here is the exception. I always announce the tip for the crew so everyone can hear it, and the dealer always makes a big deal out of accepting it; still not many people catch on.

Remember that when you are considering the size of your bets in relation to your bankroll or session budget, always remember to plan for tip money. Also remember to budget for tipping in your overall projected travel expenses. You will feel better, the crews will be happier, and your overall experience will be more pleasant.

CHAPTER 5

Your Safety In The Casino

"Because that is where the money is!" Willie Sutton, when asked why he keeps robbing banks.

"Depend on the rabbit's foot if you will, but remember it didn't work for the rabbit." R. E. Shay

"Don't worry. You're safe now. You've got nothing left to steal." Joan D. Vinge from *Catspaw*

Your personal safety is of the utmost importance, but losing all of your money so you have nothing left to steal is not the way to protect yourself and your loved ones. Remember that the lucky rabbit's foot didn't work so well for the rabbit! But it is Willie Sutton's statement of "that's where the money is" which should ring true with the casino player.

When you are walking around in a casino, you are a target because you would not be there if you did not have some money with you. And usually this is extra money that you are already planning to or willing to lose. There is always a criminal element out there looking for easy prey to make a quick score, and they are more than willing to help you part with your money.

This chapter will cover some common sense ways to help keep you from becoming the prey. Just like with the casino, you do not want to give your money away easily; you want to make it as hard as possible to get from you. Ideally, by becoming a smarter and harder target, you will prevent someone from even trying to take your money.

Sometimes criminals look like criminals and you can tell the moment you see them that something is not right. Other times they may look like your sweet little grandma from Kansas or the kid next door. When money is involved, it seems you can never be sure. The best advice is to stay alert and always try to be aware of your surroundings. Do not get so absorbed in your playing that you forget about simple safety precautions.

The first thing you should do is always try to stay sober in the casino. The free drinks are offered because the casino knows that alcohol lowers your inhibitions and causes you to make poor decisions, making it easier for the casino to help you part with your bankroll. Criminals target you after you have been drinking for exactly the same reasons. Staying sober may not be in the casinos' best interests, but keeping your wits about you will certainly be in your best interest.

If you are going to drink, please do so in moderation or at least stay with a group of friends who can be counted on to get you home safely.

Isolating you from other activities is always on the bad guy's mind, so always try to stay in public places and in groups. Criminals need to take advantage of isolated places to avoid being detected. Never be alone or in an out-of-the-way place where no one can come to your rescue. If that means trips to the restroom together with a friend, then do it. Try never to walk anywhere alone, especially out on the streets.

Always make every effort to avoid the far reaches of a parking garage. Even when the security cameras are there to record what is happening, the security guards will most likely get there after you have already become a victim. To avoid the parking garage, use the valet parking, even if you have to pay for it. You can ask a security guard to escort you to your car or up to your hotel room if needed; he will be happy to do so, as it is a basic part of his job. You should be sure to offer a tip if this service is provided, although this particular tip may be refused.

Don't be flashy with your cash at the tables and in other places. Consider leaving the bulk of your bankroll in the hotel safe when you do not need it. If you're going to dinner, you probably do not need $5,000 in your pocket.

Set up and use casino credit to take a marker at the table so you are not carrying around your bankroll. Casinos encourage this practice, and you will be able to relax a little and enjoy yourself more. You can also use travelers' checks at the cage if you would rather not carry cash. Casino credit also lets you avoid carrying large sums of money through the airport and while traveling.

Ladies, if you are carrying a purse, never set it on the floor, drape it over your chair back, or sit it in the space between the slot machines. Put the strap over your opposite shoulder, then put on a jacket or sweater on top of that, or hold your purse tightly in your lap. If you routinely carry a purse, consider purchasing one with a steel cable in the strap to prevent it from being sliced with a knife or blade.

In the restroom, be aware of stall doors which have the coat hook very close to the top of the door. Your purse can easily be grabbed from over the top of the door, and all you will be able to do is sit there and watch it disappear. Many places now put that hook on the side wall or lower on the door, and this new location is something you should be aware of to help protect your valuables.

Men, don't carry your wallet protruding out of a rear pocket, unless that is your decoy wallet, with Monopoly money in it, designed to be stolen. Keep your real wallet in a tight fitting front pocket or an inside pocket with a button or zipper on it. A rubber band around it will help prevent it from being easily slid out of your pocket.

At a craps table, arrange your chips in the tray with the higher value chips in the middle, and the lower value chips on each edge. Then if someone grabs a chip from your rail, they only get a small one off the end of the row, because it is very difficult to pull chips out of the middle of the row. Better to lose a few white or red chips off the end while distracted than a few black or purple ones!

When playing craps, always be aware of your bet locations and when and how much you should be paid. At a crowded table, especially when playing with total strangers, it is not uncommon for someone else to attempt to pick up your winning bet after it has been set in front of you by the dealer. Sometimes this may be a simple mistake, but often it is just an attempt at stealing, with the would-be thief hoping it gets overlooked in the confusion. Pick your chips up as soon as the dealer places the stack, and then if two hands reach for it, the dealer can intervene, declaring the correct owner. You might give that stranger the benefit of the doubt the first time it happens, but be especially alert after that, and watch your own chips even closer.

On other table games, when you have a stack of chips, do the same thing by always putting a few lower denomination chips on top of the higher value ones. Then if someone grabs a few, hopefully, they only get the cheap ones on top.

When you have a stack of chips, always beware of someone "tapping" them for luck with a closed fist or a drink glass. A little two-sided, sticky tape on the bottom of the glass and there goes one of your chips!

When playing the slots, do not leave a coin bucket sitting between the machines or on top of the machine, and try to remember not to walk away from it. Many machines now issue tickets, which are vastly more convenient to put away in your pocket, and are much cleaner to touch.

Now let me mention a few ideas about your own physical security and safety while staying in the casino hotel, or in any hotel for that matter.

If getting on an elevator and things just don't look or feel right, then do not get on! Trust your instincts here and do not worry about offending anyone. Your safety and security are more important than the feelings of a stranger.

If you are accosted when walking in the hotel hallway to your room, yell "FIRE" as loud as you can. That will bring people into the hallway quicker than yelling for help, because some people are not willing to get involved with helping another person out in distress. Knock on as many doors as you can to get attention.

When you are staying in an unfamiliar hotel room, take a few moments to read the safety information and get your bearings, just like when flying. During an emergency in the middle of the night is not the time to be figuring out where the exits and stairwells are located.

Never open your hotel room without looking through the peephole and verifying who is at the door. If a person claims to be a maintenance worker or other hotel employee, call the front desk and ask if the employee is supposed to have access to your room. If someone knocks on your door with a delivery or room service you are not expecting, you can always call the front desk to verify the reason and request security be present.

Any money or chips you may find on the floor belong to the casino. Do not think the chip is yours just because you found it lying there. I would not even touch it; instead call for security or other casino personnel to deal with it. I know this does not sound fair, but trust me on this point; you do not want to be arrested for stealing from a casino, no matter how innocent this act may seem to you. The exception to this rule is if a player notices that he or she dropped the money or casino chips and can prove it. If it is yours, you can pick it up.

Another variety of people (criminals) who come out of the woodwork when there is money around are those who work in the sexual hospitality industry. If you suddenly find yourself being aggressively approached by someone offering a date or company, it is probably not because of your charm and rugged good looks. It is probably because you have money on you, and your internal personnel safety alarm should start ringing! Remember, while they say that what happens in Vegas stays in Vegas, criminal arrest records and diseases will certainly follow you everywhere and you will be lucky if your wallet is the only thing you lose.

Casino security is there primarily to protect the casino from theft, but the in-house security guards will also make every effort to protect the patrons as well; they strive to prevent all types of criminal activity on their property. If something does happen to you, report it to casino security and management, and be prepared to deal with the local law enforcement organization that has jurisdiction in that area.

Gaming and gambling should be fun, and if you follow the rules and pay attention to your own personal safety, you should be able to play and stay safe while having a great time, and maybe come away a winner as well.

CHAPTER 6

Getting Comps

"Never play for comps!" Frank Scoblete, America's #1 Gaming Writer

"Never play for comps!" Every other gaming author

Complimentary items – "comps" – are things of value given to the casino player by the casino management as a means to encourage continued loyal play. Comps can be gifts to take home such as shirts and jackets, or reimbursement of money to be spent on services, such as covering the cost of a meal or hotel stay.

Jean Scott is known as the "Queen of Comps" and writes extensively about comps and how to receive them. One of her books, *The Frugal Gambler*, is all about comps and is definitely recommended reading to learn many of the details and tricks of the trade. Another great book full of comp information is *Comp City* by Max Rubin. I think this book should have been called *Max Comps*! Both of these are excellent books and you can't help but learn how to increase the comps you receive when you read them.

But the basic rule on comps is you should never play for comps. Take them if they give them to you, and you may negotiate for more and better, but never alter or increase your play strictly to increase your comps. If you budget $200 for the session and then wind up losing $475 just to get a free buffet, then you have paid a tremendous price for that meal; it had better be a great buffet. Even if you just lose a portion of the $200 trying to earn the buffet comp, it is too high a price to pay.

Never play for comps – play to win!

Two key parts of getting comps are always signing up for the casino player's card, and by asking to be rated when playing at the table games. Your play is tracked automatically when you insert your player's card into any machine. Today most play (action) is tracked by the casino, and it is usually done electronically on your player's card account.

Comps are given to the player based on the "theoretical" loss, which is what the casino projects it will win from your play using a formula based on the following four things: the number of bets you make on average per hour of the game you are playing, how much you bet on average, how long you play in hours, and the house advantage (HA) of the game you are playing. A player's level of expertise can figure into this formula as well.

After the theoretical loss is determined, then a percentage of the casino's projected win may be returned to the player in the form of a comp. Usually, this percentage is in the range of 30-50%, but it can vary significantly, depending on your value to the casino.

Here is an example of how the theoretical is determined. Let's say you are playing blackjack at $5 per hand for 2 hours. The formula would look like this (Mild math alert!): 60 (hands per hour on average for BJ) x $5 bet x 2 (hours play) x 0.02 (2% is a normal HA on blackjack) equals the theoretical, which is 60 x $5 x 2 x 0.02 = $12.

The casino is projecting their total win from you on your $5 blackjack play over two hours to be $12. *Whether you actually win or lose does not enter into this equation.*

Based on the theoretical of $12, the casino may give you back, in the form of comps, between 30-50%, which is $3.60 to $6.00, again regardless of whether you won $10 or $100, or lost the same amount. So $5 blackjack play for 2 hours is not going to get you a comp of a free night's stay anywhere, unless it is at your mother's house. At least there you might also get a free meal.

And this theoretical is based on the average player, with a 2% HA applied (for blackjack play). If the casino thinks you are an expert player, it may then apply a 1% (or less) multiplier, thus cutting your comps in half.

A bigger example of $150 blackjack play for 4 hours at 2% would give a theoretical of $720, and a 50% return (which is high) would be $360 in comps, which should cover a regular room and any food or beverages (RFB) in most casinos today. With a 1% HA used and a 30% return, this figure drops to $108, which may cover a meal in the regular restaurant or a discounted room, but probably not both.

You can always ask how your average bets are being determined, or how the casino has rated your action. For example, would playing 2 spots at blackjack for $25 per hand be considered as $50 total play or still just $25 play? Or if a pass line bet at craps of $10 with 5 times odds of $50 behind is considered a $60 bet or a $10 bet? Always ask, because the amount recorded by the pit boss makes a huge difference on your rated action. You might think you are a $60 player, and the casino may have you rated at $25, so it never hurts to check.

The projected win is just that – a projection. Remember about the house advantage from Chapter 2 when I said that the casino really does not care about short term wins or losses, or whether you are winning or losing right now. The casino really cares about the long term averages, and the theoretical is just that, an average of your projected losses over time, and not an accounting of whether you are really ahead right now or behind. Again, your actual winning or losing amount does not usually come into play when figuring the comp amount you may be entitled to.

But in reality, partly depending on your value to the casino, your short term losses may have a *slight* impact on the person writing the comp. If your theoretical doesn't warrant a particular comp, but you just dropped $750 in 30 minutes on the blackjack table, then you may get a courtesy comp to the buffet or something similar so you do not feel like you have been totally beaten. The casino would like you to be able to say you got something from them, and hopefully you will return to play again. (Never count on getting a courtesy comp, as some casinos and hosts can be totally heartless.)

On the other hand, if you're way ahead in the short term, and your theoretical doesn't warrant a free stay in the hotel, you may get it anyway. The casino might like you to stay and give them a shot at getting the money back.

Your loyalty to the casino and what the bosses believe they can win from you over the long term is what makes you a valuable commodity to them. That is why player development is a big part of the casino host's job, and why you may occasionally get a comp you haven't fully earned. The host would like you to be happy on this particular trip and return to their casino to continue playing well into the future.

By having a player's card, which is really a loyalty card, you earn and accumulate points with that casino or casino brand, just like frequent flyer miles with an airline. Usually, you will not receive many comps on your first visit to a casino, but after a few visits you will.

Player cards keep track of the points you have earned based on your play, and you can check your point balance at kiosks inside the casino or even online. Many times, you do not even need to interact with a casino host to get a comp; you just swipe your card at the register and your comp points are deducted.

How many points you are earning is a secret in some casinos and plainly displayed at others. Different games award points at different rates, so $10 bet at craps may earn you a different amount points than $10 bet at blackjack, and so on. A video poker machine might give 1 point per $10 of play, while a regular slot machine might give 2 points for $10.

It never hurts to ask what dollar level of play or for how long you need to play, in order to earn a certain comp. The comp system is multi-tiered and complicated. If you are expecting a certain comp, then you should know what the casino is expecting of you in order to give you that comp. The host will tell you that the comp you are asking for will require X hours of play at X dollar amount.

With comps, again don't forget the basic rule, which is never play just for comps. Paying the $100 tab with cash in the steakhouse is almost always better than trying to win or earn a comp for the same meal. You probably won't want to tell anyone that the $45 meal in the casino restaurant cost you $460, so please never play for comps. If you do receive a comp to the restaurant based on your play, then by all means take it, but never alter or increase your play for the free comp.

Instead of asking a yes or no question of a host, such as "Can I have a comp to the steakhouse?" try an open ended question, such as, "How long will I need to play at this level for a comp to the steak house?" Or something like, "Would you evaluate my play and let me know what I could expect in the way of a food comp?" Try to give the host some options, and the host will try to make you happy.

Loyalty to a casino is the way to accumulate comp points. If most of your play is at a specific casino or brand, then you will receive more in comps than if you spread your play around to many different casinos. But still, remember that you are playing to win and not to earn comps. If the playing conditions suggest that you should move or change casinos, then do so. Do not play at a particular casino just for loyalty's sake alone.

When you sign up for the player's card, you will begin to receive all kinds of valuable offers of free play or match play (like free money to use at the game) and free room coupons. There can even be offers of free or discounted food, special pricing for entertainment events, and coupons to pick up free stuff at the gift shop, like a t-shirt or a shot glass.

After you sign up, and the more you visit the casino, the more offers you get in the mail. Always read these carefully, and if they are offers you can use without changing the way you play, then by all means use them to your advantage. But again, always remember that you should never change the way you play just for the comps. Have you heard that somewhere before?

Ask if you and your spouse can have your cards or your accounts connected, so you are both earning towards the same account. After all you are going to share the room or the meal together anyway. Some casinos will honor this request for you if you ask.

Sometimes the values of the comps you receive outweigh the amount of money you might lose, and you become a net winner for the session or trip. Suppose that based on your play, you receive $200 in comp value in the form of free food and discounted hotel stays, and if you lost less than $200 in actual cash to receive these comps, then you are really ahead overall. Even better is when you have actually won money and still received these comps. Through careful advantage playing, this net win can happen more than you realize.

There are numerous ways to attempt to increase your theoretical, while at the same time attempting to reduce your overall risk of monetary loss to the casino. Many of these are covered in the two books mentioned earlier and in books by many other authors. This cat and mouse game you play with the casino (besides the actual physical games you are playing) can be challenging and great fun (and is completely legal) but could potentially get you labeled as a "comp hustler," which may get your comps reduced or even cut off completely.

Some of the ways to increase your theoretical while reducing your risk are as follows: bet bigger when the pit crew is watching and less when they are not looking, play slower or fewer hands per hour by various means, avoid showing expert play, and so on. There are many books out with entire chapters devoted to each of these techniques and many other ideas as well.

Most of these books will show examples of the expected theoretical based on two examples, with one using the particular technique and one not. The results (in different comps) can be amazing, to say the least, and none of them involve cheating.

Again, always remember the basic rule of comps, which is never play for comps, but do take advantage of the offers and opportunities that make sense for you. Play your game to win, and if comps come with that play, then good for you – take them, as they are icing on the cake.

Also remember that the casino is a business, and its business is to make money. If you consistently beat them, they will soon stop sending you offers, trying to lure you back to their establishment.

If you beat them enough times, the casino bosses may even ask you not to play there any longer, which is a good problem to have. I would rather be a winning player, than a favorite guest of the casino. You are only a friend to the casinos when they can regularly take your money from you.

The casino will treat you like royalty while you are losing your money. Do not fall into the trap of playing for comps because of the special treatment, especially if you are losing money in exchange for the royal treatment.

Always play to win, and never play for comps. Winning is the most fun, and trust me here; winning money from the casino is much better than a free buffet from them.

CHAPTER 7

Tips On Different Games

"Gamblers rely on luck – casinos rely on math." Unknown

"Las Vegas was built for people who are bad at math." Penn Jillette of Penn & Teller

"You cannot beat a roulette table unless you steal money from it." Albert Einstein

This chapter is not about how to play the individual casino games, because there are countless books that go into specific detail on how to play each of the different games. Rather, this chapter is designed to be an overview of the best bets within the different games, the bets that offer the lowest house advantage (HA).

By selecting games and bets within those games that have the lowest HA, you give yourself and your bankroll the greatest chance of winning, or at least losing less or losing a little slower.

All casino games have a built in HA in order for them to make a profit and stay in business, and while it is true that gamblers rely on luck, the casinos rely only on the math of the game. When you learn that you cannot fight or beat the math (the HA) in the long term, you are well on your way to becoming a more successful player.

With a little luck and correct play, you can give yourself the best chance to overcome the low HA bets and leave the casino as a winner. But always remember that while all bets will win once in a while, the higher the HA is on any individual bet, the greater the chance that the casino will win your money from you, and not the other way around.

Remember from Chapter 2 that the HA is expressed in the form of a percentage, such as 1.41%, or 16.66%, which means that (on average over time) for every $100 you wager you will lose $1.41 or $16.66, with both of these two specific house advantages being found on a craps table.

In the very short term of "right now" or "during this session", you *may* win that 16.66% HA bet once in a while, but over time and with repeated plays, you will lose it and your money *far more often* than you win it. All bets can and do win with varying degrees of probability in the short term, but these high HA bets are very hard to overcome in the long run, and they *will* eat away at your bankroll.

This is a mathematical certainty that you can take to the bank: you cannot overcome the HA.

So If we know we are always going to lose to the HA, then why make the bets with the higher HA? It is because it's exciting to win them and the short term payoff is much larger, but you need to know that the expected (and predictable) long-term impact is that your money will become the casino's money.

The following are some thoughts and tips on the best and most popular games found in casinos today. The emphasis is on the HA you will be up against, as well as how to play to allow your bankroll to last as long as possible and, thus, have a fighting chance of winning.

Now two more things. You should not play any casino game that you do not understand; not knowing what you are doing in the casino is deadly to your bankroll. You should never play at a game when you don't know the impact of the HA on your bankroll, or when you don't know the most player-friendly bets to make, or when you do not know what it takes to win.

And secondly, if you are playing in tournaments, you should know that the game strategies and betting patterns to win may be much different than for normal casino play. Make sure you understand the differences before you enter the tournament, especially if you have your money on the line.

BLACKJACK:

In blackjack, the house advantage runs from less than 0.5% with good, player-friendly rules, to a high of just over 2% with the more casino-friendly rules.

But the reality is that poor play alone often results in a *self-imposed* HA of 15-20% or more! The casinos don't beat you; you are beating yourself and handing over your money without a fight.

Blackjack can be one of the very best games in the casino if you play it correctly, and one of the worst if you don't.

The best advice for blackjack is to learn the correct basic strategy and then stick to it. *Never* deviate for hunches, or because the last time you made a certain play you lost. The basic strategy is the time-tested and proven model for correct play in each situation or with each dealer up card.

Most blackjack experts say that only a very small percentage of players learn and follow the basic strategy. Instead, most play by the seat of their pants and follow superstitions, hunches, habits, and bad advice from fellow players.

Every blackjack book in print has this basic strategy information in it, and you can usually even buy a small plastic basic strategy card in the casino gift shop. Most casinos will not mind if you lay the card on the table to refer to while playing, but be sure to ask first. Sometimes the dealer will ask that you place the card on your lap and not on the table.

This is a good place to say that you should not offer any unsolicited advice to the other players at the table. If they ask for advice, then it is up to you if you want to give it or not. Also remember that other players' poor strategy play will help you just as often as it hurts you, so don't get too bent out of shape when the player at third base takes what would have been the dealer's bust card. You can always move to another table.

By learning the basic plays and the required deviations, you will be on your way to becoming a formidable blackjack player whom the casino fears.

I believe that 95% of your improvement in Blackjack play can be made simply by learning and following the optimal basic strategy (with the other 5% coming from learning a simple card counting strategy). You should be aware that there are many different basic strategies, depending on the number of decks and rules of the individual game. Find and learn the one for the game you usually play.

Not all blackjack games are created equal. Always look at the rules of the game (printed on the table layout or table placard) to see if this particular game is the best one being offered. Maybe the game offered on the next table over is better for the player. Most casinos will offer a few different variations of the rules on neighboring tables, all with a different HA.

Look for games with player-friendly rules that allow the player the most flexibility or advantage, such as splitting aces, re-splitting, doubling after a split, dealer stands on all 17s (S17), early and late surrender options, allowing doubling on more than 2 cards, and for tables that pay 3:2 for a natural blackjack.

Each rule that is good for the player will decrease the HA by a small amount and will sometimes add up enough (subtracting from the HA) to make it a nearly even game, or at the very least, a much better game for the player.

Less favorable rules for the player are allowing a dealer to hit a soft 17 (H17), only allowing doubling on a 10 or 11, no splitting of aces, and 6:5 payouts on natural blackjacks. While these rules increase the HA by a small amount, the 6:5 game is a deal breaker. Never sit and play at a 6:5 game. When your $5 bet that has always paid $7.50 for a natural, now only pays $6 for the same win, you should vote with your feet and find a different game. The casinos win plenty from poor play alone, and this rule just adds insult to injury.

All other things being equal, fewer decks are better than more decks, so a single-deck game dealt by hand is more favorable than an eight-deck game dealt out of a shoe. Usually, you give up some of the more favorable rules to have a single-deck game, so you should evaluate the total picture before deciding which game to sit and play at.

Avoid side bets and carnival game variations of blackjack, such as Spanish 21, Lady Luck, Double Exposure, and 21 Madness. This extra madness really just adds extra HA for the casino.

After learning and using the basic strategy, if you really want to take your game to the next level, you will need to learn a simple card-counting strategy.

The basic premise in card counting is that it provides you some information as to when you are more likely to win your hand, as well as when you are less likely to win. If you then know that some hands are probably going to be better for you than others, you can adjust your bet size accordingly.

The theory is that you bet more in situations where you are more likely to win and less on the hands you are more likely to lose. Card counting allows you to make that decision before you place your bet, and learning to count cards is not nearly as hard as the movies would have you believe.

One of the easiest methods is the Speed Count, and you can find it in *Beat Blackjack Now* by Frank Scoblete. A 12-year-old can learn this simple counting method; and once you learn it, you will have a proven mathematical edge. And of course, the optimal basic strategy for the Speed Count is included in his book as well.

All card-counting systems do work, with the emphasis on work. Most are usually mind-numbingly hard work for a *very* small extra edge. And while card counting is completely legal, the casino is constantly on the alert for the card counter, as they know that their small HA or edge can easily shift into the favor of the skilled counter. The Speed Count is exceptionally easy to use, and it does not look like normal card counting, so the extra scrutiny from the casino does not usually come, which is a good thing. Try it – you'll like it.

As I said earlier, most of your improvements (I believe 95% plus) in play will be found by simply learning the correct basic strategy for the game you are playing. That step alone will separate you from the masses of Blackjack players who are mindlessly handing over their money, and put you on the path to becoming a formidable, winning Blackjack player.

Insurance is the sucker's bet in blackjack, assuming you are not counting cards and know when it is beneficial for you to take this bet. You are paid 2:1, which gives a HA of over 7% on it. Taking even money instead of insurance is exactly the same thing and should also be avoided.

The main advantage that the casino has over the player in the Blackjack game is the simple fact that the dealer gets to play last. If you draw and bust, you lose, even if the dealer then busts as well. You play first, and when you bust, the dealer picks up your cards and your bet, and you are done for the hand before the dealer even plays. It is not a tie when you both bust, because you bust and lose first. Always remember the game is to beat the dealer, not to get as close to 21 as possible.

The advantage to the player is that you are allowed many choices as to how to play your hand, including options to put extra money into play on good hands by doubling and splitting. You also win more money on natural blackjacks, while the dealer wins even money. The player can also decide to take extra cards in an attempt to beat the dealer's hand when needed, while the dealer is bound by fixed rules on drawing, even when he can plainly see that he is beaten.

On average the dealer will win 48 out of every 100 hands, the player will win 44, with the remaining 8 becoming pushes. So, in order to come out ahead when you actually lose more hands overall than you win, you need to capitalize on these 44 hands by winning as much money as possible on them. This is where following the basic strategy becomes of utmost importance; showing you exactly when to put extra money into play with correct splitting and/or doubling down plays.

Time spent learning the correct strategy for hitting, splitting and doubling will pay tremendous dividends in your ability to win more from the casino.

CRAPS:

Craps is an exciting, communal game with around 40 or more different bets available to you. When you hear a loud cheer in the casino, it is coming from a craps table. If you are looking for me in the casino, look at the craps table (or in the restaurant).

The example of 1.41% to 16.66 % at the beginning of this chapter comes from the craps table. Some of the best bets in the casino can be found on the craps table, as well as some of the worst.

A general rule of thumb is that any bets you hear the dealers reminding you to make will carry a high HA, while the very best bet, the odds bet, is not even marked on the layout.

Both the pass line and come bets have a HA of 1.41%, with 'don't pass' and 'don't come' each at 1.37%, making these bets the best ones to put down on the craps table.

Taking odds on these bets reduces the HA even more. The 'odds bet' has no HA against it and is the very best bet on the craps table. Because there is no built-in HA, the odds bet dilutes downwards from the HA of the bet it is placed with. So a pass line bet that normally has a 1.41% HA will now have a 0.61% HA with double odds, but you also have more of your money (three times as much) on the table being exposed to the HA. 10 times odds reduces (dilutes) the pass line HA to 0.19%, and 100 times odds will reduce the pass line HA to 0.02%.

Just remember that with increased odds, you are also exposing a larger portion of your bankroll to the casino, and your $5 pass line bet with 10 times odds is now $55 on the table, so make sure your session bankroll is large enough to support this level of play. While odds does lower the HA, it also increases the variance, or monetary swings you will experience.

Most casinos have 2X odds or 3-4-5X odds or 10X odds (some offer 100X or more). The odds are posted on a placard on the table along with the other table limits. The general rule of thumb is always play the maximum odds allowed in order to have the lowest HA applied to your money.

The next best bet is placing the 6 or the 8, which will have a 1.52% HA.

Buying the 4 or 10 will have a 1.67% HA (on tables where the commission is paid on the only win), while placing the 4 or 10 will expose you to a 6.67% HA.

The pass line bet with odds, or come betting with odds, or placing the 6 and/or the 8, or buying the 4 and/or the 10 will all provide you with the best chance of beating the casino, while exposing you to a HA of 1.67% or less. Don't start out on all of these numbers right away; instead, go up on them gradually. (See the fifth paragraph down from here.)

These are the best bets to make on the craps table, and all others should be avoided. The other bets will cause you to lose your money between three and twelve times faster because of the increased HA. Any book on Craps will have a table showing the different bets and HAs that you will be playing against.

The sucker bets on the craps table are the Big 6 and the Big 8, each of which pays even money when won. By simply placing the six or eight, you get paid 6:5 if won; therefore a $10 bet on the Big 6 or Big 8 pays $10 if won, while the same $10 bet placed on the six or eight pays $12. This Big 6 and Big 8 bet is so bad for the player that it is not even allowed in Atlantic City, but you will still see it offered on the layouts most everyplace else.

The center bets (proposition bets) all carry a HA of 9.09% to 16.66% and should be avoided as well.

Okay, I know you are still going to make these bad bets anyway, so here is what I recommend: set aside a very small portion of your session bankroll to make these crazy bets with. Take $5 or so out of every $100 and then only make these high HA bets with that money. This way you still get to play them once in a while (with everyone else), but you do not expose your entire bankroll to these unacceptably high HA risks.

Always remember when playing craps that you win your bets one at a time, but you lose them all at once. The player who places multiple bets right away is fighting an uphill battle from the beginning. When you have bets on many of the numbers, you will need to win one more bet than the number of bets you have up in order to be a net winner. So a pass line bet and four other numbers will require five wins to break even and a sixth win to be ahead. (I know this doesn't account for the payout odds - this is just a generalization.) Again, the point of this is that you win your bets one at a time, but you lose them all at once.

I recommend going up on numbers gradually after you win the first few bets you place. If a player winds up having a long roll, you will be up on it, while protecting your bankroll from the quick seven-out.

BACCARAT:

Baccarat is a very simple game with set rules and methods of play. The only real option is how you bet, and then there are only three choices: the banker wins, the player wins, or a tie (push).

The HA for a bet on the player is 1.24%, while the HA for a bet on the banker is 1.06%. The 5% commission (or Vig) is only collected on banker wins (with a 4% Vig, the HA drops to 0.60%), and the lower HA reflects the slight advantage the banker has over the player. Over time the banker will win slightly more often than the player.

The advantage is always for the banker, as the banker gets to play last. If the player draws a third card and improves the hand, the banker will draw in an attempt to beat it. If the player draws a third card that does not improve the hand, then the banker does not need to draw again.

Avoid betting on the tie, because the HA is 4.84% or 14.36%, depending on if the payout is 9:1 or 8:1 respectively.

The sucker bets here are any side bets and the tie when the payout is at 8:1.

If you like a quiet, dignified game for high stakes (table minimums are usually $25-100 or more) where you dress up in nice clothes to play, then Baccarat could be your game. I would rather watch paint dry.

Mini Baccarat is the same basic game with lower betting limits played on a smaller table. It is a much faster game in decisions per hour, and you may actually wind up exposing a larger amount of your bankroll to the casino in this format.

PAI GOW POKER:

Pai Gow is a fun game to sit with your friends and socialize. It is played very slowly, so you do not expose your bankroll to the casino at an overly fast pace, and the HA is one of the lowest, at 2.54% when you are the player and even less when you are the banker.

In addition to the slow play and the low HA, more than 40% of all hands usually end as a push (neither the player nor the banker wins), so no money changes hands, making this game even better to play. Remember that a *copy* (banker and player having equal hands) is different than a push, and results in a win to the dealer.

Because close to half of the outcomes result in a push with no money changing hands, actual wins and losses occur much less frequently here than in other table games. Sometimes you can play for hours with very little overall monetary change to your bankroll, while still earning comps.

Mathematically, both the player and the banker have the same probability of drawing winning cards, with the advantage swinging to the banker because of copies.

If your bankroll will allow it, you should always be the bank whenever the opportunity is made available, but remember that as the banker, you will need to be able to cover as many as six other bets.

With the advantage to the banker, the recommendation is to bet larger when you are the banker and less when you are the player.

This game can result in 27 different types of hands, but around 90% of them fall into one of the following six types: no pair, one pair, two pair, three pair, three of a kind, and a full house. By learning just the correct plays on these 6 hands, you will be playing the best way nine out of ten times. Then you should try to learn the entire basic strategy (the house way), and follow it.

ROULETTE:

Roulette is a very popular game in the casinos. While the HA is high at 5.26%, the game itself is played relatively slowly (with fewer decisions per hour in relation to other games), so it is not that bad to play. The only advantage to this game is that it exposes your bankroll to the casino much more slowly than other games.

There are two different styles of wheel: the American wheel with both a 0 and 00 with 38 total pockets, and the European wheel with only a single 0 and 37 pockets. The American wheel has a HA of 5.26%, and the European wheel with only one house number (the 0) has a HA of 2.63%.

The simple advice here is always attempt to find a single 0 European wheel to play. This is much easier said than done however, as usually the only place to find these wheels is in the high limit areas. Still, it never hurts to look.

If you do find a European wheel, check to see if the casino offers any kind of rules allowing second chances if the ball lands on the house number of 0. While rarely offered, these rules reduce the HA by one half again, making this game the very best you can hope for.

The sucker bet on the regular American wheel is the "first 5" bet on the 0 & 00, and 1, 2 & 3. This bet has a HA of 7.89%, and it should be avoided. All other bets and combinations of bets have the normal high HA of 5.26% and are better than this particular bet.

There is no betting strategy, system, money management, or method of play (on an unbiased wheel) that will allow you to beat roulette, no matter what others may tell you. The HA of 5.26% is constant and will eat away at your bankroll.

Remember that roulette chips are only for the roulette table. Do not carry them away with you and attempt to use them anyplace else. They do not have value denominations printed on them, and each player gets his or her own color to use at the table. The value is determined by the amount you buy-in with, and the roulette dealer will cash them back out for you in the same manner as you bought in.

VIDEO POKER:

Video poker is extremely popular, and there are many different versions of machines, such as Jacks or Better (JOB), Bonus Poker or Double Bonus Poker, and Deuces Wild.

Some have a 99.9% payback (or higher) depending on the skill of the player, and the skill of the player is the key to success, as expert play is required to have any fighting chance at all.

Each game has its own strategy, *and playing like you do in the poker games at home is not it*. Some of the required plays are not at all intuitive and require a great deal of study to master.

Find and buy a computer tutorial that simulates the game or games you like, and play for free at home until you are proficient.

Video poker is much more predictable and beatable than regular slots because the Random Number Generator (RNG) strictly simulates the probabilities of dealing from a freshly shuffled deck of cards. You do not need to worry whether or not this is a tight machine or a loose machine because everything is in direct relation to the make-up of an actual deck of playing cards.

Extra jokers or wild cards change the probabilities in exactly the same way as if you were playing with them in a regular deck of cards at home. The true odds are fixed, and only the payout odds vary with the pay tables.

All payouts are determined by the various pay lines on the printed pay table, so the real Video Poker strategy becomes trying to find the games with the best pay tables.

The tutorials and different books available will all go into the different games and pay tables in great detail, so I will only give an example here.

The basic example that is always used is the pay table from Jacks or Better (JOB) with the main payout variations showing on the Full House and Flush lines.

These are discussed as if they are represented by a fraction, such as 9/6. The 9 represents the number of coins returned for each coin bet for a Full House and the 6 is the number of coins returned for each coin bet for a Flush.

With JOB 9/6, the return is 99%, for a 1% HA.

With JOB 8/5, the return is 97%, for a 3% HA.

With JOB 6/5, the return is 95%, for a 5% HA.

It is not unheard of with expert play for some machines to return 100.2% or more, so the real trick is finding the machine with the best pay table. Often you will see two similar machines that are side by side but have different pay tables, thereby giving them different HAs.

There are 40-50 (or more) different variations of Video Poker around, with a payback percentage anywhere from the low 90s to over 100%, and as I said before, expert play is required to get to the higher percentages.

Find a few games that you like, and then use a computer simulation to learn the strategies to play them correctly.

SLOTS:

Slot machine play is extremely popular, and accounts for a large percentage of all of the money won by the casino. Most slots pay back to the player between 83% and 99%, with the average being in the low 90s, meaning that the HA on slots runs from 1% to 17%, and usually averages out to around 8% to10% or so.

Casino advertisements around slots might say something similar to "Pays up to 99%", with the "up to" part usually in very small print. What these signs really mean is that one of these machines will in fact pay up to 99%, but it does not mean that all of the others do. There may be a group of machines in a circle being advertised with one of them paying back the full amount and the others being closer to the average or less.

One thing to be aware of when playing slots is "churn", which means to play your wins back through the machine in hopes of winning even more instead of setting the wins aside. With coins it is easy to place the wins into a coin bucket and, thus, keep the amount won separate from the buy-in; but with credits and the TITO (ticket in / ticket out), wins simply add to your credits, and continuing to play becomes very easy.

For example, if you start with $20, and play all the way through it, you will have about $18 left because of the small wins you will have. Then, when you play through that amount, you have about $16.20 left, again with the casino retaining about 10% on each churn of your money. After 15 to 20 rounds, or churns, you find that your $20 is completely gone.

The casino has won 100% of your money, but only about 10% at a time. *This is the expected outcome with continued play*, while in the short term you may in fact win from time to time.

You will have numerous small wins and near misses as you play, and it will seem as if you are very close to the big win or jackpot. Those small wins and near misses will cause you to want to continue to play, or churn, your money through the machine, resulting in the long-term expectation of your bankroll disappearing into the hands of the casino.

The best you can hope for is to figure out which of those machines are the ones with the higher paybacks. They are deliberately not marked as such, because if they were, no one would play the others. If you frequent the same casino, over time you may notice that one does in fact pay better than the others, but do not let the short-term wins affect your judgment here, as it may take months to really figure out which are the good machines.

All other things being equal, the higher the denomination of the machine, the better the payback percentages. Nickel machines pay better than penny machines, quarter machines pay better than the nickel ones, and so on. This extra payout percentage may be measured in a fraction of a percent, so do not over play your bankroll here looking for this small extra edge.

Make sure to understand the pay table and especially know if there is an advantage for playing the max coins. On some machines the payback is linear and pays back exactly in relation to the amount of coins played, while other machines will increase the payback with increased coin play.

Often these machines will increase the payback only on the final coin, so look at that in relation to your bankroll. If there is a benefit to playing maximum coins, make sure your bankroll can support that play.

As a general rule, you will be better off playing the maximum number of coins on a machine you can afford than playing fewer coins on a higher denomination machine. It is usually better to play five nickels on a nickel machine than it is to play one quarter on the quarter machines. It is the same 25 cents, but you gain the max coin advantage this way.

Also be aware of playing max coins *and* max lines. Some penny machines may take $3.50 to $5.00 or more per play (25 cents times 20 lines is $5).

Most of the primary win benefit on slot machines is found in the bonus rounds, so make sure you know how to get there and how to play when you are there. Play the least amount of money that will allow the bonus to kick in. The most benefit on multi-line machines can usually be gained by playing the max number of lines and often without the max coins. This will give you the best chance of bonus, with the least amount of money per spin.

Slot machine owners are very competitive with pay back percentages in crowded markets. You will find the best paying machines in areas where there are multiple casinos in close proximity to each other. The other side of this story is that casinos in locations with limited competition have less incentive to provide good paying machines. It may be the only game in town (or state) but you do not have to play there – it may be better to save up for a trip to another location.

Slot machines are the junk food of the casino. We know they are bad for us, but we just can't help ourselves when we are around them. And like junk food, they are best taken in moderation. You really have very little control when playing a slot: you put your money in, and you take your chances.

At least when slot machines had a handle to pull, it made sense to call them one-armed bandits. The "button pushing" bandit just doesn't have the same ring to it! But at least you can control the speed at which you hand over your money to the casino by pushing the button a little slower.

So the best advice when it comes to slot machines is to find games you like, learn how they work, and then play them very slowly to get the most entertainment value in relation to the time spent in the casino.

CHAPTER 8

Paying Taxes

"The Internal Revenue Code is about 10 times the size of the Bible – and unlike the Bible, contains no good news." Don Rickles, Comedian

"The hardest thing in the world to understand is the income tax." Albert Einstein

"You must include your gambling wins in income." IRS Publication 17

In this chapter, I will attempt to give an overview of what the IRS intends when they say in Publication 17 "You must include your gambling wins in income," and hopefully provide some guidance as to what this statement means to everyday players when making decisions that will affect their wallet.

As always with matters involving your individual personal income tax, you should seek out the expertise of a competent tax professional. Hopefully you can find someone who is well versed in the nuances of reporting gambling income (hopefully you will have gambling income). The best you could hope for is a tax pro who is also a successful, winning gambler, and if you do find such a person, please forward his or her name to me.

First let's talk for a moment about Al Capone who spent most of the final years of his life in prison for tax evasion. We remember him as a Chicago-land gangster who led a 1920s prohibition-era bootlegging and prostitution crime syndicate and who was an all-around bad dude. But those activates are not why he went to the big house. He went to prison after being convicted of failing to report income to the IRS, not for his other criminal enterprises. Even though everyone at the time knew what he was doing, the only thing they could make stick was tax evasion.

While income tax *evasion* is certainly illegal, income tax *avoidance* is as American as apple pie and is probably most of the reason why we even have tax professionals. Anyone who has any type of income is obligated under our current taxation system to pay taxes on that income, but no one is required to pay the maximum amount suggested by the government. With good records and tax preparation, you can (and should) pay only the minimum required amount.

So remember, income tax evasion is highly illegal, but income tax avoidance is highly encouraged.

Those who would like to read in depth on this subject are encouraged to order *Tax Help for Gamblers* by Jean Scott and Marissa Chien. It is a great book full of useful information as well as plenty of fine print for those of you who can't live without all of the details. I recommend you get a second copy for your tax prep professional as a gift; it couldn't hurt and will probably save you some money in the long run!

Here is the deal: all gambling income is (should be) reported as income and is fully taxable. Now for the fine print (remember – the large print giveth, and the fine print taketh away) your losses can be deducted only up to the amount of the reported winnings, and then only if you itemize your deductions. Any losses you have in excess of any winnings *cannot* be used to offset any other income.

If you got lucky last year and won $3,000 someplace, and then throughout the rest of the year you wound up losing a total of $5,000, you can only use $3,000 of the loss to offset the $3,000 in winnings – and you lose (again!) the ability to use the other $2,000 lost as a deduction.

You claim your gambling losses as a miscellaneous deduction on your IRS Form 1040, Schedule A, line 28. You can refer to IRS Publication 529, Miscellaneous Deductions, for more information.

If you take the standard deduction, and do not itemize your deductions, you do not get to use any of the $5,000 in losses as a deduction and must (should) still report the entire $3,000 in winnings as income on your IRS Form 1040, line 21.

The IRS Publication 525, Taxable and Nontaxable Income, will provide additional information and guidance.

In order to use any deductions, you will need to be able to document them, so it is important to keep an accurate log, diary, or similar record of all of the relevant information. You will need to record your net win or loss per session, as well as any other information that can substantiate your statements.

Your log should include as much information as possible, such as: the date, time, venue, location, game, table or machine number, the buy-in amount, the cash-out amount, time played and anyone who was present.

Also, this log might include any other proof that this information is true, such as airline tickets, hotel room invoices, ATM receipts, show tickets, and meal receipts as well as any IRS Form W2-Gs that you may have been issued (which will be covered later in this chapter). I tend to go a little overboard in my log because I do not want to argue with the IRS about anything that I claim.

As a casual recreation player and not a professional gambler, you can declare only the actual wins and losses you have experienced and not any other incidental expenses that you may have incurred, such as tips or travel expense. The items that you document in your log or gambling diary are only to provide support for the wins or losses you are claiming. Pro gamblers should consult a good tax professional for advice.

Did you notice I said "per session" above? What is a session according to the IRS? As with the rest of the gambling guidance provided by the IRS, they are a little vague, but they do require that you "net out" your win or loss *per session*. I am sure that a session is not last year or last weekend, but that it is a smaller period of time that you play, such as the afternoon session or the evening session.

So while it would not be okay to say that you won $3,000 and lost $5,000 last year (for a net session loss of $2,000), it would be okay to record that you bought into the afternoon session for $500 and cashed out two hours later for $300, for a net loss of $200, and so over a three day trip to Vegas you may have six to ten or more different playing sessions. I would define a session as every time you bought into a table or pit area, played for a while, and then cashed out and left.

If you are playing at a blackjack table, and you get up and move to another table in the same pit, I would call that move a part of the same continued session. After all, who doesn't do that from time to time when the dealer is being bad to you. But if you pick up your chips from the blackjack table and go over to the craps pit, I might be inclined to start calling that a new session. Gambling is supposed to be fun and not a record-keeping exercise, but the more accurate you keep your log or diary, the better shape you will be in at tax time.

What about slot players who jump from machine to machine? Surely you would not be expected to record 25 sessions before breakfast, another 53 sessions that afternoon, and then 47 more after dinner, for a total of 125 sessions. (That would be a bunch even for the most dedicated slot player!) But I do think this day could show three sessions in your log, and I think anyone could defend this position to even the most hard-hearted IRS auditor. Some would say this entire day is one session, and while I understand that position, I would not want to have to defend it.

My definition of a session is relatively short periods of play, separated by breaks to do other things like swimming, sleeping, or eating (mostly eating for me). I think a session can be anywhere from an hour or less up to an entire morning, afternoon, or evening. Maybe a poker player would play one session for a day or longer, but I do not think a session is a trip, a weekend, or a year. Just remember that you and/or your hired tax help may have to defend your definition of a session sometime in the future, so be as accurate as you can.

At the end of the day (and tax year), an accurate log or diary is your best defense and will probably help you save some money on the taxes you owe from all the money you and your buddies won on the big bender in Vegas.

As a side note, gambling losses are gambling losses. All of the money that you dropped at the track on the ponies, all of the non-winning lottery tickets you bought, all of the sports book wagers you lost, and all of the money you left in the casinos is considered gambling losses as far as the IRS is concerned.

The type of gambling loss does not come into play, and you do not have to use a particular type of loss to offset a particular type of a win. Just keep track of all the wins and losses in your log so you can get the full benefit of your losses when you complete your tax returns. Hopefully, your log will not become part of the evidence in some type of a family gambling intervention.

What about when the casino issues you a W2-G? Well, congratulations. This usually means that you had a slot win greater than $1,200. The W2-G is for "Certain Gambling Wins" (written right on the front of the form), and lists on the backside the four times that it is issued: 1) $600 or more in gambling wins and the payout is at least 300 times the amount of the wager (except winnings from Bingo, Keno, and slot machines), 2) $1,200 or more in gambling winnings from Bingo or slot machines, 3) $1,500 or more in proceeds (the amount of winnings less the amount of the wager) from Keno, and 4) any gambling winnings subject to federal income tax withholding.

Did you notice on #2 that it was $1,200 in "gross" winnings on slots (from a single spin), while on #3 it was $1,500 of "net" winnings for Keno. This #2 is the reason that you will see slot machines advertise payouts of $1,199 in order to cut down on paperwork!

This win paperwork takes time to complete, and you cannot put more money into the machine, as the slot machine is locked out after a win over $1,200. After the W2-G is issued, a slot technician will need to open and reset the machine for continued play.

What is absent from the list on the W2-G is winnings from table games, such as Blackjack, Roulette, Baccarat, 3 Card Poker, Craps, and others. Because you buy-in and make bets in these games for different amounts, it is much more difficult to determine the amount of your winnings on the spot.

Only when the payout on a single bet is $600 or more, *and* it paid off at 300:1 ratio or higher are W2-Gs issued for these games. Some examples of this might be progressives on Caribbean Stud and Fortune Pai Gow as well as some bonus bets on Let It Ride.

Because no W2-G is issued for table games, many people erroneously believe that they do not have to report these types of winnings as income. When they have a win, they think that the casino doesn't report it, so why should they. If you think this way, I would refer you to the example of Al Capone in the beginning of this chapter. Remember all gambling wins are reportable.

Playing is fun, and winning is the most fun, but not when you lose sleep at night worrying about if the IRS will be knocking on you door at some time in the future. Always remember what your mother told you, "Honesty is the best policy." Always play to win, and when you do win, report that money as income.

CHAPTER 9

When Gambling Becomes A Problem

"The urge to gamble is so universal and its practice so pleasurable that I assume it must be evil." Heywood Broun, American Journalist and Novelist

"There are two times in a man's life when he should not speculate: when he can't afford it and when he can." Samuel Clemens as "Mark Twain"

Addictions come in many forms – such as tobacco, alcohol, drugs, spending, sex, and gambling. Do you know the warning signs of problem gambling? The following 15 questions have been developed by Gamblers Anonymous and others to help individuals determine if they may have a gambling problem. Read them and honestly ask yourself if they may pertain to you.

Have you been restless or irritable when unable to gamble?
Have you hidden your gambling from family members?
Have you missed important appointments to gamble?
Have you had issues at work because of your gambling?
Have you been unable to pay bills due to gambling losses?
Has a loved one questioned your gambling?
Have you hidden your finances from others?
Have you tried to stop gambling but have not been able to?
Have you gambled to obtain money to pay debts or solve other financial problems?
Have you ever diverted needed household money to gamble with?
Have you ever needed someone else to bail you out of a gambling debt?
Have you ever borrowed money and not paid it back as a result of your gambling?
Have you ever thought you might have a gambling problem?
Has gambling created conflict and unhappiness in your life?
Have you been distracted with thoughts of gambling while doing other things that require your attention?

If you answered "yes" to any of the questions, you may be at risk for developing a gambling problem. The more questions that you have answered in the affirmative, the greater the likelihood you already have a gambling problem.

At almost every casino I have ever been to, there is a brochure readily available with information on how to obtain help. The casinos do not want you to become a problem gambler, and they will attempt to help if you ask.

Gamblers Anonymous is available most everywhere there are casinos, and is there to help if you need it. It can be found at www.gamblersanonymous.org, and they also have a hotline telephone number in almost every state.

Another source of help is the Problem Gamblers Help Line at 800-522-4700 for confidential information and assistance. The Help Line is a free service of the National Council on Problem Gambling, and is available 24 hours a day. Counselors will answer your questions, send you information, and direct you to the resources in your area.

As a side note, if you know you have a problem gambling, you can voluntary have your name placed on the exclusion list at the casino, and then the security staff will refuse to allow you to enter or play.

When the line between fantasy and reality becomes blurred, it is time to stop. You may dream of winning every trip and being a high roller receiving all of the comps and accolades, but the reality is that the casino is in a business to separate you from your money. While there may actually be a free lunch at the casino from time to time, at the end of the day, someone has to pay the bills. Remember that there are always going to be more losers than there are winners.

Maybe you don't cash out as a winner every time, but hopefully you are still cashing in on the fun of playing. Gambling is supposed to be fun, but please stop playing when it begins to cause problems or is no longer enjoyable.

CHAPTER 10

In The End
The Hold Is What Matters

"When the casino takes all of your money, then the HA is really 100%." Missouri Rick

"The casino calls it gaming, but you ain't gaming – you're gambling." Max Rubin, Gambler & Author

When you ask, "Why did I lose most of my money when the HA is only 2-5%?" you are really asking about the hold, and not the HA. The amount of money the casino *actually* wins or retains each day from every game is called the hold. While the HA may be low on many games, the hold is often expected to be 15-20% or more.

The HA pays the bills and keeps the lights on for the casino, but the hold provides the real profits. As we saw in Chapter 2, the HA is mathematically designed to provide a relatively small edge to the casino on each and every bet, but that small HA doesn't account for all of the people that get wiped out in the casino.

The hold is defined as the amount of money actually retained by the casino on each game. So if a particular table game takes in $10,000 for the night (the drop) and pays out $8,000 in chips, then the difference is the amount the casino actually wins on this game on this particular night. In this example, the hold (or retained amount) is $2,000, or 20%. The HA on this table game may only be around 2%, but the amount won by the casino is 20%, 10 times more than the HA.

Slot machines are designed with a HA of between 1 and 17% (99-83% payback), and while most really average between 5-8% HA (due to competition among the casinos), the hold runs in the 10-16% range (around double the HA). But on table games, the hold will usually run between 5 to 10 times the HA. It is not unusual for Blackjack, Roulette, or Craps games to have a hold in the 20-25% range of the total drop or cash taken in.

The HA is the amount that the casino knows they will win from the edge built into every bet, but the hold is what it actually wins for a variety of reasons. While there are many bets with a low HA, there are many more with the HA running 11.11% to over 25%! Most people, hoping for a big win, will continuously replay, or churn, their money through those bets until they are broke.

The casinos want you to think that it is indeed possible to walk in off the street with a few hundred dollars and walk out as a multi-millionaire! When that rare event does in fact happen, it makes all of the headlines around the world.

The casino provides the opportunity – and the adult entertainment casino experience – and people line up to hand over their money.

Casino marketing is phenomenal and is constantly studied and tested to see what works and what doesn't.

Everyone has heard the expression, "What happens in Vegas stays in Vegas." The marketing and tourism guys are still drooling over that phrase. But what about these phrases: Only take what you can afford to lose, The HA is the cost of admission, and Vegas wasn't built on winners?

You may even remember reading all of these expressions in this book, but really, the above phrases help to instill the fact that you are going to lose, and that it is socially acceptable. Today, millions of people enjoy going to the casino. When Grandma is going to gamble at the casino and there is no longer a social stigma attached to it, then that is marketing at its best.

I am sure somewhere there is a room full of casino marketing experts trying to figure out a way to get you to just mail them your money – or better yet – just wire it to them, maybe with Pay Pal.

While there are many ways the casino helps you gladly part with your money, the main way is just through poor playing. People go into a casino without a plan of attack and with a poor understanding of how the games are played. You do not really need to know all of the finer details on a particular game, but you should at least know the basics of how you lose and what it takes to win.

With the books and computers available today, there is no reason for anyone to go to a casino unprepared to win; both a little study and a little practice are needed before you go. Just because you played 21 as a kid doesn't mean you are ready to take on a casino Blackjack game with your money, and Video Poker is not the same as the poker games you sit in on back home. Street Craps is much different than casino Craps. At least slots are just slots; you put your money in, push the button, and then wait for the machine to tell you if you won or not.

The very best advice is to figure out the games that you like to play in the casino, and then locate a book or two on those games and find out how to win at them. People buy a multitude of books about chess or golf, and every other game under the sun, and those games are not usually played for money. It just makes sense to read a Blackjack book if you are going to wager your money on the outcome.

Again, you do not have to study for an advanced degree in those games, but at least find out the basic strategy and what it really takes to win. Then you will have the knowledge to become a formidable adversary to the casino; a player who has to beaten for his money.

While the player brings a casual attitude and poor or weak play to the table, the casino does the following and much more to help you part with your money.

Did you ever notice that there are no windows or clocks in the casino? Being inside, you can easily lose track of time, and you often do not know if it is the middle of the afternoon or the middle of the night. What time is it? It's happy time! Enjoy yourself and keep playing. There is no rush to leave; the casino never closes.

The casino wants you to feel that way; it never wants you to feel like you've been playing too long and it's time to leave. Casino design is an art unto itself: *everything* is done for a reason, and that reason is to make it easier for you emotionally and physically to leave your money in the casino.

Most casinos offer hotel rooms and restaurants throughout the property. They want to ensure you stay at their property for as long as possible and continue to play and churn your money through their games. There is no reason to go home, for the casino has everything you need.

The alcohol is free, and it is the casino's best friend. When you are stone cold sober, would you bet your entire paycheck on rolling a 12 at the craps table or on hitting 22 black on the roulette table? Of course not, but after countless free drinks, you are probably not making rational decisions any longer. You keep on playing, and the casino will keep bringing free drinks until you are busted.

The cocktail waitresses are often dressed very seductively, and they are much friendlier than you would expect. They work for tips, and they are more than happy to be your friend and bring you free drinks, as long as you keep on tipping.

The noise in the casino can remind you of a carnival where everyone is happy and having a good time. The constant noise is amazing when you try to listen to the individual sounds. Bells and whistles, buzzers and ringing, all going on 24/7.

I like the sound of coins dropping out of a slot machine into the tray. It sounds like you are breaking the bank, and it is made to sound this way on purpose. If car manufacturers can make cars quiet, don't you think the casino could make slot machines quieter? But that noise is one key part of keeping you at the machine and attracting new people to play because it sounds like everyone is winning.

I really like the sound of the newer ticket-in / ticket-out slot machines where there are no coins, but they still have the pre-recorded sound of coins dropping into the tray with a win.

The ticket-in / ticket-out slots also make it very easy to keep playing because now you are only spending credits and not real money. You cannot set your wins aside in the coin bucket to save – because there are no coins. Before you even realize it, you have played through all of your credits.

Near misses on the slot machines make you want to keep on playing – because you were SO close to hitting the jackpot. You think the next spin will be luckier, so you keep on playing, and the many small wins only encourage you to keep on trying.

The different slot areas are often located in a smaller, somewhat secluded area to give you a safe and secure feeling. Again, by design.

The carpets are hideous and make you look up away from them. The ceilings are equally unattractive, and make you look down. The only thing left to look at are the games in front of you. There are also usually no long, straight sight lines. Instead there are many pit areas and curved aisles.

The layout in the casino is designed like a maze on purpose. It is remarkably easy to find your way in, but not nearly as easy to find your way out again. I guess we should just stay and play since we are lost in there anyway; the casino counts on you feeling that way.

Most of the time, to get anyplace in a casino, you have to walk through the gaming area. The restaurant is past the Blackjack pits. Going to the pool from your room – turn left at the Roulette table. The elevator is near the Craps tables, and the slots are close to everything. Finally, to cash out, you will find the cage in the very back, past all of the games.

Comps are designed to keep you playing a little longer to get the next better complementary. Genius. And the Players Club makes it even easier to give all of your money to one casino brand.

The person who first decided to play for chips (and credits) instead of real money should win a Nobel Prize. When $25 is a small piece of green plastic and called a "quarter," it doesn't seem so bad to toss it out there. After all, it is play money, not really $25. Red $5 chips are called "nickels." If you had to put a real one-hundred dollar bill down to bet, you might think twice before you did it, but it is easier when it is just a black plastic chip. Again, genius.

There is an overwhelming amount of red color everywhere in the casino because red is associated with power and winning. The general lighting is typically soft and subdued, never bright or harsh.

The list of design features goes on and on. Everything in the casino is well thought out and designed to make you comfortable, relaxed and happy. *Nothing* is left to chance.

The main way the casino helps you part with your money, though, is by showcasing the high HA bets and counting on you to not know better. As I said before, the casino is counting on you to come to the casino with a casual attitude and for you to have poor, near-continuous play until you have no money left.

The casino is always the home team, and you are always the visiting, "away" player. It is designed to be an overwhelming game in which you have very little chance of winning. They want you to be entertained and to have a good time, but mostly they want you to leave your money behind with them.

Some people do win from time to time on luck alone, and that is purely gambling, but many more lose. By learning what it takes to win, and by becoming a smarter casino player, you can dramatically increase your chances of winning, while at the same time lowering the hold of your money to the casino.

Figuratively speaking, the deck is truly stacked against you in the casino. They would never cheat you with a real stacked deck; they do not need to. The HA and the hold take your money completely legally, with your help, of course.

At the end of the book, Missouri Rick says, "Stop helping the casino!"

With a little knowledge of the games, a proper bankroll, good money management, a good game plan, and a little luck, you can become what the casino fears the most; a winning player who knows how to beat the casino at its own game. Good Luck.

CHAPTER 11

Glossary

What It All Means

"Get the facts first – you can distort them later." Samuel Clemens as "Mark Twain"

Action – The amount of money a player wagers over a period of time. It can also be used to state the size of a player's average wagers, as in "His action is $25".

Advance Fee Fraud – Promising a victim a large sum of money if they invest a small amount of money. Also referred to as a 419 (the US Criminal Code covering this type of fraud).

Advantage play – Using correct basic strategies at blackjack, strategy cards at video poker, making only low house edge wagers, comp hustling and/or using any other legal way to gain a slight mathematical edge over the normal casino house advantage.

Advantage player – Someone who is very knowledgeable or skilled in advantage play, and who may then have a slight advantage over the casino in certain games.

All-in – To bet your entire stake or bankroll.

American wheel – In roulette, a wheel that has both the 0 and the 00, with a total of 38 slots for the ball to land in. See also "European wheel".

Amulet – As a superstition, can be any small object but its most important characteristic is its alleged power to protect its owner from danger or harm, or to bring good luck. See also "talisman".

Anchor position – In blackjack, the position nearest the dealer's right is "third base" and will be dealt to and played last, and is sometimes referred to as the anchor position. See also "first base" and "third base".

Any craps – In craps, a one roll bet that the next throw of the dice will result in a 2, 3, or 12.

Any seven – In craps, a one roll bet that the next throw of the dice will result in a 7, also referred to as an "Any" or "Skinny".

Angle shooting – Refers to legal but possibly unethical ways to attempt to beat certain casino games, such as taking advantage of weak dealers who may flash hole cards or make erroneous payouts. As in "I look for and take advantage of all of the angles".

Ante – Poker players each "ante" a small amount of money to start an pot to be won at the beginning of each new hand, for the privilege of playing in that particular hand. This is different from the "rake" which goes to the house. Ante is Latin for "before".

Apron – On a craps table, the plain unmarked outer edge of the table layout.

Arm – In craps, a person who is highly skilled in tossing the dice.

Arm – In slots, the lever attached to the right side of the machine to activate play.

Astragalomaney – The practice of divination by use of dice.

Automatic shuffling machine – Automatic card shuffling machines shuffle the cards to be ready for the next round of use in a game, as opposed to hand shuffling, which reduces the number of hand played per hour. See also "continuous shuffle machine".

Backline – In craps, another name for the Don't Pass Line.

Back counting – In blackjack, involves watching the play of cards in a game without actually wagering your own money, until the count becomes advantageous, and then stepping in and playing only while the count remains in the player's favor, and then stepping out again. Back counting or "Wonging" is the reason that some casinos have signs on some blackjack tables saying, "No Mid-Shoe Entry," meaning that a new player must wait until exactly the first hand after a shuffle to begin playing. After Stanford Wong who made the technique famous. See also "Wonging".

Back hand – In pai gow poker, the five card high hand placed closer to the player. Can also be called the high, behind, bottom, or big hand.

Back the bet – In craps, placing free odds on the line bet is referred to as "backing the bet".

Backtrack – In roulette the outer rim of the wheel where the ball spins. It is also known as ball-track.

Bad beat – Losing with what is, or appears to be, a considerably stronger hand.

Bank – Entity or person covering all of the bets, usually the casino.

Banco – In roulette, the banker.

Banker – A card came banker is someone who books the action of the other bettors at the table, and may be the casino or another player.

Banker hand – In baccarat, the second of the two hands dealt.

Bankroll – The amount of money a player sets aside to gamble with, also called a "stake".

Bankroll, Emotional – The amount of money you can afford to lose painlessly, which will not affect your lifestyle or make your hand tremble.

Bankroll, Fixed – A onetime bankroll that will not be replenished.

Bankroll, Replenishable – A bankroll with no fixed money amount, as a specific amount of money is always being re-deposited into your bankroll, such as a percent of your paycheck each pay period, and thus never runs dry.

Bankroll, Session – The amount of money available for a specific session of play, and is a percentage portion of your trip bankroll.

Bankroll, Total – The entire amount of your gambling funds.

Bankroll, Trip – The amount of money available as a bankroll for a specific trip, which will cover multiple sessions of play, and is a percentage portion of your total bankroll.

Bankroll management – Choosing the correct stakes and game type to avoid exhausting one's bankroll during downswings.

Bar – To refuse service to a player.

Bar the 12 (or the 2) – In craps, "baring the 12" (or 2) means that on the come out roll, an outcome of a 12 (or a 2) results in a tie for the player betting the "don't pass" and "don't come".

Barney – Slang for purple $500 chips.

Barring – When casino personnel permanently restricts or prohibits you from playing a particular game, or any game in the casino.

Barber pole – A wager make with a stack of various color chips mixed together, and is not appreciated by the dealers, as winning bets must be resized prior to being paid. Also referred to as a "dirty stack".

Base dealers – In a crap game, the 2 dealers who stand on either side of the Box man, facing the players, who collect and pay all bets. Also a name for card cheats who deals from the bottom of the deck.

Basic strategy – In blackjack (21) the basic strategy the set of plays that provide you with the maximum advantage; or the best moves to make in order to play the most correctly for the given game which will give you the best chance of winning.

Beginner's luck – Refers to the supposed phenomenon of beginners experiencing a disproportionate frequency of success.

Benjamin – Slang for a $100 bill (Benjamin Franklin is featured on the note). See also "C-note".

Bet (or wager) – The amount of money that is risked on the outcome of an individual event, and is sometimes called a wager.

Bet spread – The range in the size of bets in a series of bets, as in "I spread my bets from $5 to $30".

Betting Limits – On a table game, the betting limits establish the minimum and the maximum amount that can be wagered on any one hand. This amount may change during the game as the conditions or times change in the casino.

Betting systems – Techniques to beat a game of chance by changing the amount of the bets, which do not work.

Bias – When an outcome is no longer random.

Biased wheel – In roulette, a wheel that favors particular sections as a result of an improper setup placement or a manufacturing flaw.

Big Mitt – Slang for a fixed or rigged poker game.

Big Red – Nickname for the seven during a crap game, since the 7 on its betting space on the layout is usually large and red, and it is considered bad luck and a breach of etiquette to speak the word "seven" at the table. See also "Any-7" and "Skinny".

Binary bet – A bet with only 2 possible outcomes of win or lose, with no possibility of a tie or push.

Black Book – A complied list of individuals from Griffin Investigations in the form of a book who are generally suspected to be (or known to be) either an outright cheater at the casino games, or an advantage player. These individuals are blacklisted from the casinos who subscribe to the service, as they are perceived to be a threat to the casino's profit. Also referred to as the "Griffin Book".

Black chips – $100 chips are usually black in color.

Blank – In keno, the blank ticket used to mark selected numbers.

Bleed – Consistently losing chips through bad play, possibly resulting from tilt. When a player is consistently losing chips, they are said to be "bleeding chips".

Bluff – In poker, is a bet or raise made with a hand which is not thought to be the best hand.

Board – In keno and bingo, the electronic sign displaying the numbers called while the game is in session.

Board – In poker, the community cards in a hold'em game.

Boat – Slang name for a full house in card games.

Bones – Slang word for dice, as in "roll them bones".

Bookie – A person who collects and pays off the bets that are made.

Bottom Track – In roulette, the inner area of the wheel that slants or remains stationary, where the ball slides before bouncing from the wheel onto the pocket.

Bowl – In craps, the wooden or plastic container near the stickman that the dice rest in.

Box – The center section of a craps table layout where the proposition bets are made.

Boxcars – In craps, when a 12 is rolled (two 6s) it is often called "boxcars" (slang) or "midnight" (slang – referring to 12 o'clock).

Boxman – (or Box person) This person is the craps table supervisor who sits between the two standing base dealers and opposite the stickman. The Box man receives and counts out a new player's money when entering the game. In addition to overseeing the entire game, he is responsible for watching the winning payouts at the end of the table opposite where the dice landed, which are being watched by the stickman. This salaried casino job is referred to as "sitting box" and does not rotate out on breaks as the regular dealing crew does. He may or may not share in the tips (tokes) at the table.

Boys – In craps, slang for the dealers.

Break the deck – In blackjack, when it is thought that a card counter is at the table, an early reshuffle is sometimes called "breaking the deck", in order to break the count. See also "preferential shuffle".

Break the bank – The rare event when a gambler wins more money than the house has on hand.

Bricks – Shaven or misshaped dice that are no longer random. See also "flats".

Brick & Mortar – A brick & mortar or B&M casino is a "real" casino based in a building, as opposed to an online casino. This refers to many real world locations vs. their Internet counterparts. It is not just a poker term or even a gambling term; it is often used in e-commerce in similar situations.

Broke money – Money given by the casino to a player, who has lost everything, to pay for transportation home.

Brown chips – $5000 chips are usually brown in color. See also "Chocolate chips".

Buffalo bet – In craps, slang for a combination bet on all four hardways plus the any-7.

Buffalo yo – In craps, slang for a combination bet on all four hardways plus the 11.

Bullet – Slang for an Ace.

Bunco – Slang for a trick, scam, scheme or con that deceives people into parting with their money.

Burn card – In cards, after shuffling and cutting the deck, the first card is discarded, and is called the burn card.

Bust – In blackjack, a total greater than 21 is a losing hand, and is said to be "busted". Also when a player has depleted (lost) the entire buy in or gambling stake, he is said to have "gone bust!"

Buskers – Slang name of the numerous street performers in Las Vegas.

Bustout dealer – A crooked dealer employed by an after-hours club or illegal casino. This dealer is brought into the game to get rid of a customer who is problematic, or to make sure a player does not walk out with big winnings.

Button – In poker, the white disk placed next to the player who is considered the dealer for purposes of order of play.

Buy bet – In a crap game, buy bets may be used instead of place bets, and they are paid at true odds, but a 5% commission (vig) is charged on the amount of the bet. The opposite of a "Lay bet".

Buy in – The amount of money required to join a game, or the converting of cash into chips at a table game, is said to be "buying in".

C note – Slang for a $100 bill. See also "Benjamin".

Cage – The casino "bank teller window" where you can turn your chips (called checks) back into cash, and where you may sometimes cash actual checks, getting cash or chips to wager with.

Call – In poker, to match another player's bet. See also "see".

Called bets – In roulette, these are bets that cover a certain area of the wheel rather than the set bets on the board. These bets are not offered in all casinos.

Camouflage – Techniques used to diminish the appearance of advantage play.

Candle – On slots, the name of the light on the top to alert a slot attendant that the machine needs attention of some sort.

Cans – Slang for the drop box which serves as a repository for cash, markers, and other receipts on a gaming table.

Capping – A form of cheating by adding additional chips to the top of a bet stack of chips (opposite of a pinch).

Card counting – Card counting means keeping track in your head of some running summary statistic (a running count) that gives you some meaningful information as to which cards have already been played, and thus not available to be played again. This then, allows you to infer which cards may be coming next so you can adjust your bet size and playing strategy to your advantage.

Card guard – A chip or small object place on top of cards, to prevent another player's discards from winding up in the hand by accident.

Card mechanic – A card cheat who specializes in sleight-of-hand and manipulation of cards, also known as a card sharp.

Card shark – An expert card gambler who takes advantage of less-skilled players.

Card sharp – A professional card player who makes a living by cheating at card games.

Carousel – A group of slot machines in a circle or a ring.

Cash back – As a comp, receiving a portion (or rebate) of your money back.

Cash out – To go to the cage and redeem your chips for cash is called "cashing out".

Casino advantage – The casino advantage or edge is the percentage of each bet you make that the casino takes in or retains. In order to get this edge, the winning wagers are paid out at less than true odds. It is regarded as the price you pay to play, or as an entertainment tax. See also "house advantage" or "HA".

Casino hold – Is the percentage of all player's money won by the casino.

Casino night – Fund raising entertainment events with a gambling or casino theme, usually at a location other than an actual casino.

Casino rate – A discounted casino hotel room rate, often offered to good customers if you ask for it.

C&E bet – (Craps & Eleven) - In craps, a bet on 2-3-12 & 11.

Center bets – These are the wagers made on the center part of the craps table layout (the box area), and are often referred to as proposition bets.

Chance – An informal term for probability.

Change only – When players put money on the table to get gaming chips.

Chasing – Increasing your bets in an attempt to regain earlier losses.

Cheating – Is any behavior outside the rules that is intended to give an unfair advantage to one or more players.

Check – In poker, declining to bet.

Check chopping – Stealing by palming a chip.

Check raise – In poker, is to check and then raise on the same round of betting. See also "sandbag".

Checks (Cheque) – Another term for chips.

Chip – A round gaming token (usually of clay, plastic, or metal) to wager with instead of using actual cash.

Chip tray – The chip tray holds that table's inventory of chips.

Chipping machine – In roulette, the machine that sorts the different color chips for the dealer.

Chocolate chips – $5000 chips are usually brown in color, and are often called "chocolate chips".

Choppy – In craps, slang for a table having inconsistent Passes and Misses with no good runs of winning throws.

Chung – In pai gow poker, the marker indicating the dealer's hand.

Churn – To constantly re-bet your stake.

Closing line – The final point spread or line given in a sports book before the contest begins.

Cocked dice – In craps, when one or both dice come to rest leaning against another object, and therefore are not sitting flat on the table surface. The number is determined by what the outcome would be if the object were to be moved, showing how the dice would fall.

Coin bucket – Plastic cup used to carry coins for slot play.

Coin hopper – In slots, the internal container that holds the coins that are immediately available for payouts.

Coin tray – In slots, another name for the drop bucket (or tray) that collects and holds coins that are paid out.

Cold – A condition where players perceive that a trend is not favorable and losing will continue.

Cold deck – Is a deck of playing cards arranged in a preset order, designed to give a specific outcome when the cards are dealt, and which is typically switched with the deck actually being used in the game in question, to the benefit of the player and/or dealer making the switch.

Collusion – Is when two or more players are acting with a secret, common strategy. Some common forms of collusion are: *soft play*, that is, failing to bet or raise in a situation that would normally merit it, to avoid costing one's partner or friend money; *whipsawing*, where partners raise and re-raise each other to trap players in between; *dumping*, where a cheater will deliberately lose to a partner; and *signaling*, or trading information between partners via signals of some sort, like arranging their chips in a certain manner.

Color up – A player leaving a game will often place all of his chips on the table and ask to "color up". The dealer will count the chips and then give you back the same amount in larger denomination chips so it will be easier to carry them to the cage to cash in. For example it is much easier to carry $300 as 3 black $100 chips, than it is to carry the same $300 as 60 red $5 chips.

Columns – In roulette, on the betting layout there are three columns with 12 numbers each. To bet a column is to wager that one of those 12 numbers will win.

Combination Bet – In roulette, using one or more chips in the same position to bet on more than one number simultaneously.

Combination ticket – In keno, a single ticket where the player has marked at least two groups of number that form several combinations that allow more "ways" to play. See also "way ticket".

Come bet – In craps, a come bet can be visualized as starting an entirely new pass line bet, unique to that player. A player making a come bet will bet on the first point number that "comes" from the shooter's next roll, regardless of the table's round.

Come-out roll – When playing craps, the rolls before a point is established are referred to as come-out rolls.

Commission – The percentage retained by the casino on winning bet. See also "house advantage".

Community cards – In poker, the cards placed face up in front of the dealer, and used by all of the players.

Comp hustling – Those who play games with a low house advantage may attempt to get more in free items (comps) from the casino than their expected monetary loss (or actual losses), and is another form of advantage play.

Comps (Complimentaries) – Casinos sometimes issue complimentary gifts (comps) to entice a player to gamble, or to reward players for gambling. Typical comps include free room (R), food (F), and beverages (B). These 3 are referred to as RFB. Many other items of value can be comp'd as well, such as small or large gifts, show tickets, or even airfare.

Complementary Event – The event complementary to a given event is the set of all possible outcomes that are not the given event (or are not in, or do not represent, or do not satisfy the set that is the given event). For example when playing craps, one event could be: "The total of both dice is 7" and the complementary event would be: "The total of both dice that is not 7".

Confidence game – (also known as a bunko, con, flim flam, grift, hustle, scam, swindle or bamboozle) is an attempt to defraud a person or group by gaining their confidence. The victim is known as the mark, while the trickster is called a confidence man (con man, grifter, or con artist) and any accomplices are known as shills.

Continuous Shuffling Machine (CSM) – Automatic card shuffling machines which shuffle the cards continuously during a game. See also "automatic shuffle machine".

Cooler – Mythical employee of the casino who is said to have the ability (just by his presence) to change a player's short term luck from that of being a winner to being a loser, and thus stopping a winning streak.

Copy – In pai gow poker, when both the player and the banker have the same value hand.

Corner bet – In roulette, a bet placed on the corner where four numbers meet, and which pays 1/4 the win of a single number.

Count down – Process where a dealer forms smaller stacks of chips from a lager stack, in order to count them.

Crapless craps – A craps game variant where 2, 3, 11, and 12 are point numbers.

Craps – Is a dice game in which the players make wagers on the outcome of the roll, or a series of rolls, of a pair of dice. Players may wager money against each other (street craps, also known as shooting dice or rolling dice) or a bank (casino craps, also known as table craps). Because it requires little equipment, street craps can be played in informal settings.

Crapping out – When playing craps, the shooter craps-out (or throws craps) by rolling a 2, 3, or a 12 during a come-out roll, losing his pass line wager, along with everyone else who has the same wager in place.

Credit line – The amount of credit made available to a player by a casino.

Credit meter – In slots, is a visual display of the amount of money or credits available to play on the machine.

Crew – The casino employees who work a craps or baccarat table.

Cross-roader – An older slang name for a casino cheat.

Coup – In roulette, one roll or one decision.

Croupier – A French word for the dealer. In roulette, the dealer is called the croupier (pronounced croop-EE-ay).

CTR – Currency Transaction Report - A report that U.S. financial institutions are required to file for each deposit, withdrawal, exchange of currency, or other payment or transfer, by, though, or to the financial institution which involves a transaction in currency of more than $10,000.

Cut – After a deck of cards is shuffled by the dealer, it is often given to a player for a procedure called a cut. The dealer completes their shuffle, and then sets the cards face-down on the table near the designated player, typically the player to the dealer's right. The player cuts the deck by removing a portion of cards from the deck, and places them toward himself so that the stack of cards to be dealt is closest to the dealer. The simplest form of the cut is done by taking, roughly, the top one-half of the cards, and placing them on the table or a cut card. Either the player cutting or the dealer then completes the cut by placing the remaining bottom portion on top of the cards that have been cut off.

Cut card – A plastic card similar in size of a playing card, usually bright and solid-colored, placed by a player into the deck to indicate where the dealer should cut the cards, and on hand dealt games, is then held against the bottom of the deck after the cut by the dealer to prevent observation of the bottom card during the deal.

Dark side player – In craps, a dark side player (wrong side or don't player) is betting that the pass and come bets will lose; as opposed to the "right bettor" who is betting that the pass and come bets will win. Both are correct ways to play.

DAS – in blackjack, abbreviation for the rule allowing Doubling After Splitting.

Daub – A paste or material used by card cheats to secretly mark playing cards, usually while the game is in progress. See also "luminous reader".

Deadwood – Slang for the pile of playing cards that have been discarded. Also a gaming destination in South Dakota.

Dealer – The casino employee who operates a table game.

Deuce – Slang for a two in a deck of cards, or the side of a die with two pips on it.

Dice – Two or more identical numbered cubes with multiple resting attitudes used for generating random (in the sense of lacking predictability) numbers or other symbols. 6-sided numerical dice are used in craps. Dice is the plural of die.

Die – A traditional die is a 6-sided cube with a different number of circular patches or pits on each side called pips. The design as a whole is aimed at each individual die providing one randomly determined number in the range of 1 to 6, with each of those outcomes being equally likely (unbiased or fair). The six sides of a die are called ace, deuce, trey, cater, cinque and sice.

Dirty money – Chips in a losing bet that have not been returned to the rack by the dealer, but are used to pay other winning bets.

Dirty stack – A wager make with a stack of various color chips mixed together, and is not appreciated by the dealers, as winning bets must be resized prior to being paid. Also referred to as a "barber pole".

Discard tray – The tray or holder on the dealer's right that holds the cards that have been played or discarded, awaiting the next shuffle.

Dog – Short for the underdog, which is the predicted loser in an event.

Dollar – Slang for a $100 black chip – and is a very rarely used term.

Dolly – In roulette, the name for the marker used to mark the winning number.

Don't player – In craps, a don't bettor (wrong side or dark side player) is betting that the pass and come bets will lose; as opposed to the "right bettor" who is betting that the pass and come bets will win. Both are correct ways to play.

Double down – In blackjack, when you double down you place both of your cards face up and place an additional wager beside your original wager up to the amount of your original wager, and then you receive 1 more card face down. After the dealer plays, your card is reveled to determine the outcome.

Double duke – A form of cheating in card games, where the cheat will stack two hands, with one player getting a strong hand and the cheater getting an even stronger one. This is called a "double duke".

Double hand poker – Another name for Pai Gow Poker, because of two hands played.

Down – When playing craps, some bets may be removed from the table while the game is in play by telling your dealer to "take you down", off of the specified bets. See also "off".

Dozen bet – In roulette, a bet on the 1st dozen numbers (1-12), the 2nd dozen (13-24), or the 3rd dozen (25-36).

Dragon hand – In pai gow poker, when there is an empty seat, the dealer may deal an extra hand for the players to bet on, thus having two hands in play. The dealer sets this hand according to the house way.

Draw – In cards, to have additional cards dealt to your hand.

Drop – Term for all of the money placed into the drop box.

Drop box – The drop box serves as a repository for cash, markers, and other receipts on a gaming table. There may also be a toke box for dealer tips. Also called "cans".

Drop bucket – In slots, another name for the coin tray that collects and hold coins that are paid out.

Drop in – A new player who is not one of the regulars who usually plays in a reoccurring game or location.

Duck – Slang for a two in a deck of cards, or the side of a die with two pips on it.

Dump – When a table game loses a large amount of money to the players during a session, it is said to have "dumped". Also used as a derogatory term for a low end or run down casino, as in "This place is a dump".

Early surrender – In blackjack, the rarely seen rule allowing players to surrender their hand, and lose 50% of the wager, *before* the dealer checks the down card. This is a player friendly rule. See also "surrender".

Edge – Slang for an advantage, as in "I had the edge over him." Also short for the house edge or advantage.

EDR – Employee Dining Room.

EGM – Short for Electronic Gaming Machine, which is another term for a slot machine.

EMFH – Every Man For Himself.

Eighty-sixed (86'd) – Slang for being banned from a casino. As in "I was eighty-sixed from the Stardust when I was younger."

ETIS – Eye In The Sky.

En prison – In roulette, on a single 0 wheel (European wheel) your even money (only) bet can be returned to the player if the ball lands on "0" (the bet is placed "in prison" and not into the bank – you haven't lost it yet!) and then if the next spin results in what you initially bet, you receive the wager back, instead of losing it to the bank. This is a mostly unknown rule that is very player friendly, and effectively cuts the house advantage in half, from 2.70% to 1.35%. See also "La partage".

European wheel – In roulette, a wheel having only a single 0, with a total of 37 slots for the ball to land in, and is sometimes called a French wheel. See also "American wheel".

Even money – A bet that pays you back the exact amount you wagered (plus your original wager) and is referred to as 1:1 (1 to 1). An example is a pass line bet at craps, or a bet on Red or Black in roulette. In blackjack, taking even money when you have a natural blackjack (an ace & a 10 value card) when the dealer shows an ace insures that you win some amount. No matter the dealer's hole card, you win even money.

Event – The set of possible outcomes for a trial. For example when playing craps, one event would be: "The total of the dice is 7." This event would have six possible individual outcomes – 1 & 6, 2 & 5, 3 & 4, 4 & 3, 5 & 2, and 6 & 1.

Expected Value (EV) – The predicted future gain or loss is called expectation or expected value and is the sum of the probability of each possible outcome of the experiment multiplied by its payoff (value). Thus, it represents the average amount one expects to win (it can be negative number) per bet when bets with identical odds are repeated many times.

Expectation – The same as the "expected value".

Expected win rate – The expected win rate is a predictable percentage of your total wagers that you can expect to win or lose over time, usually expressed per hour or per $100.

Eye in the sky (EITS) – The surveillance video system or cameras that monitor the gaming areas, most public places, and any money handling areas in the casino.

Face cards – The jack, queen, and king of any suit of cards.

Face up/down – Cards that are dealt face up so everyone can see them, or down so the value is only known to the card holder. In blackjack, the player can touch cards dealt face down, but is not allowed to touch them when dealt face up.

Fade – To cover a bet in a private game.

Fair – The ideal situation in which the probability of any of the possible outcome is the same. A similar term is unbiased.

Fair game – A game or situation in which the expected value for the player is zero (no net gain nor loss) is called a fair game.

False shuffle – Appears to shuffle fairly but a selected group of cards remain in the same order. This is done with either all or some of the cards, and is a form of cheating.

Favorite – The expected winner of an event. See "underdog".

Fifty yard line – In craps, the middle of the table where the stickman stands.

Fill – When extra chips are brought to the table.

Fire bet – In craps, before the shooter begins, some casinos will allow a bet known as a fire bet to be placed. A fire bet is a bet of as little as 1 dollar, made in the hope that the next shooter will have a hot streak of setting and getting many points of different values. As different individual points are made by the shooter, they will be marked on the craps layout with a fire symbol. The first three points will not pay out on the fire bet, but the fourth, fifth and sixth point made will pay out at in increasing amounts – usually 25:1, 250:1, & 1000:1.

First base – In blackjack, the position nearest the dealer's left hand is referred to as "first base" and this spot will be dealt to and played first. See also "third base".

Flat betting – Betting the same amount on each and every hand, regardless of changes in conditions.

Flats – Dice that have been slightly shaven on one side to increase the chance of certain numbers appearing more frequently. See also "bricks".

Flat top – A slot machine with a fixed jackpot that does not increase.

Flea – A derogatory slang term for a low level bettor.

Field bet – In a crap game, is a wager that one of the numbers 2, 3, 4, 9, 10, 11, or 12 will appear on the next roll of the dice. Also referred to as a "Ladies bet".

Fifth street – In poker, the round of betting after the fifth card is dealt.

Floating craps game – The term floating craps refers to an illegal operation of the dice game craps. The term 'floating' refers to the practice of the game's operators using portable tables and equipment to quickly move the game from location to location to stay ahead of the law enforcement authorities.

Floor Person – A casino employee who supervises several table games in a pit, and who reports to the pit boss.

Flop – In poker, the first three community cards dealt face up in front of the dealer.

Fold – A card player folds a hand by tossing in (facedown) his or her cards, and thus gives up any claim on the pot in exchange for not having to add any additional money into the pot.

Fonzi scheme – Investing one leather jacket, on the promise of getting two in return. (Sorry – I couldn't help myself.)

Foreign chip – A chip from another casino.

Foul – A hand that is disqualified.

Free odds – In craps, since odds bets are paid at true odds (with no HA – thus free odds), in contrast with the pass line which is always even money, taking odds on a minimum pass line bet lessens the house advantage compared with betting the same total amount on the pass line only. A maximum odds bet on a minimum pass line bet often gives the lowest house edge available in any game in the casino. However, the odds bet cannot usually be made independently, so the house retains an edge on the pass line bet itself.

French wheel – In roulette, another name for the European wheel with a single 0.

Front hand – In pai gow poker, the two card hand, placed closer to the dealer. Can also be called the small, low, top, hair or minor hand.

Frontline – In craps, another name for the Pass Line.

Front money – Money the player brings into the casino and which is then deposited into the cage that the player intends to use for gaming purposes are referred to as front money.

Fronts – In craps, a pair of fair dice that are identical to the crooked ones.

Fruit machine – The term for slot machines in Great Britain.

Full pay – In video poker, the highest paying form of a given type of machine.

G man – Slang for a federal government agent.

Gaff – A device used for cheating.

Gambler's conceit – Is the fallacy where a gambler believes they will be able to stop a risky behavior while still engaging in it. This belief frequently operates during games of chance, such as casino games. The gambler believes they will be a net winner at the game, and thus able to avoid going broke by exerting the self-control necessary to stop playing while still ahead in winnings. This is often expressed as "I'll quit when I'm ahead".

Gambler's fallacy – This argument is that "in a random selection of numbers, since all numbers will eventually appear, those that have not come up yet are 'due', and thus more likely to come up soon." This logic is only correct if applied to a system where numbers that come up are removed from the system, such as when playing cards are drawn and not returned to the deck. In this case, once a jack is removed from the deck, the next draw is less likely to be a jack and more likely to be some other card. However, if the jack is returned to the deck, and the deck is thoroughly reshuffled, a jack is as likely to be drawn as any other card. The same applies in any other process where objects are selected independently, and none are removed after each event, such as the roll of a die or a coin toss. Truly random processes such as these do not have memory, making it impossible for past outcomes to affect future outcomes.

Gambler's ruin – A gambler playing a negative expectation game with a limited bankroll will eventually go broke against an opponent with an unlimited bankroll.

Gambling – Is the wagering of money or something of material value (referred to as "the stakes" or "the bet") on an event with an uncertain outcome, with the primary intent of winning additional money and/or material goods.

Game theory – Game theory is the science of analyzing contests to develop optimal strategies.

Garden bet – In craps, a rarely used slang name for the field bet.

Giving odds – In craps, when you have made a don't pass or a don't come wager, you can back it up by giving odds (placing additional money on the original wager) after the point has been established. This allows you to get more money into play without increasing your expected loss; however it will increase the variance you experience. See also laying odds.

George – A slang (positive) term for player who is generous and tips the dealers.

Ghost – In slots, a blank stop (spot) on the wheel.

Glimmer – Any kind of a shiny object, used to see the value of a face down card as a form of cheating. See also "shiner" or "twinkle".

Going light – When a player doesn't place the full amount of a bet into a pot, he is said to be "going light." If he wins the pot, he does not need to make up the light amount, but if he loses the pot, he then owes that amount to the winner of the pot.

Going paroli – Another term for parlaying a bet.

Going south – Hiding or removing some of your chips (into a pocket or purse) off of a table game to give the appearance to the dealer of having lost more than you actually have, and is considered to be bad form. Also referred to as "rat holing".

Gorilla – In blackjack team play, the Gorilla is the big bettor called in to play and make big bets when conditions turn very favorable to the players.

Green chips – $25 chips are usually green in color, and are often referred to a "quarters" or "greens".

Green numbers – In roulette, the numbers 0 and 00 have a green background, and are therefore called the green numbers.

Griffin Book – A complied list of individuals from Griffin Investigations in the form of a book who are generally suspected to be or known to be either an advantage player or outright cheater at the casino games. These individuals are blacklisted from the casinos who subscribe to the service as they are perceived to be a threat to the casino's profit. Also referred to as the "Black Book".

Grifter – A practitioner of confidence tricks or scams, known as a con man.

Grind – Small play.

Grind joint – A low end casino that caters to the low roller.

Grinder – Is a player who makes most of their income from playing poker (or other games) in a style that slowly allows wins at a consistent pace, as in to "grind it out". See also "rounder".

Gross gaming revenue – The amount a casino earns from games of chance before taxes, salaries and other expenses are paid -- the equivalent of "total sales," not "profit."

Gutted – To lose your entire gambling stake in a particular ugly fashion, as in "The tourist was gutted in that game by the sharks!"

H17 – In blackjack, the rule where the dealer takes another card (hits) on a soft 17. This is a casino friendly rule. See also "S17".

HA – Short for the "house advantage", and is what pays the bills for the casino. See also "house edge".

Hand – The cards held by the dealer or the players, or the individual round of a game.

Hand held – in cards, a game where you can touch or pick up the individual cards.

Hand mucking – Refers to a form of sleight of hand where a player conceals a card in his hand, and if used in a card game, is one type of cheating.

Handicapping – Handicapping involves using available information to assign a probability of winning to a sports team or an event, performed by a handicapper. This is referred to as developing "the line".

Hard count – The activity in which hard money (coins) are counted, in a special room under tight security.

Hard hand – Any blackjack hand that does not contain an Ace valued at 11 is a hard hand, such as a 6-8 is a hard 14. A hand with an Ace can be hard if the hand totals 12 or more and each Ace is valued at 1, such as a 4-10-A, which is a hard 15. A hand where the Ace can be valued two ways is a soft hand, such as a 4-A, which can be a 5 or a 15, and another card can be received without fear of busting (going over 21). Any hand totaling 11 or less is not a hard hand, because another card can be received without fear of busting. See "soft hand".

Hard ways – In craps, any even point number that is made by throwing the same number on both dice, such as a 4 as 2-2, a 6 as 3-3, an 8 as 4-4, or a 10 as 5-5.

Hayseed – Slang for a sucker.

Heads up – Playing alone against a dealer or another player. Also referred to as head to head play.

Heat – Slang for being scrutinized very carefully by casino management whole playing. See also "sweating the money".

Heater – When a player has an unusually large winning streak or session, it is called a "heater", and is a relatively rare occurrence to be celebrated.

Hedge bet – A second offsetting bet, designed to cover the loss of another bet if won (to minimize the overall loss), as in to "hedge your bets".

Hi-Lo – In blackjack, a traditional method of card counting.

Hi-Lo bet – In craps, a one-roll bet on 2 and 12.

Hi-Lo-Yo bet – In craps, a one-roll bet on 2, 12 and 11.

High hand – In pai gow poker, the five card hand closest to the player, also called the back hand. Can also be called the behind, bottom, or big hand.

High roller – A high roller is a big better, although this is relative to the size of the casino organization or operation. A person who may be a high roller at a small casino with small table limits might not even be noticed at a large casino with high table limits. A very high roller is also sometimes referred to as a "whale". Also the name of the new Ferris wheel in Las Vegas.

Hit – In blackjack, to receive another card is referred to as "taking a hit" or "hitting". The card received is also referred to as the hit card.

Hobo bet – In craps, betting on the 12. See also 'boxcars".

Hold – The amount of money retained by the casino on a particular game.

Holdout – A mechanical cheating device which allows a card to be held out of play.

Hole card – In blackjack, the dealer's unseen card that is dealt facedown is the "hole card". The player is not supposed to know the value of the hole card until he or she has played his or her own hand. In other words, the player goes first without knowing the total value of the dealer's hand. In other card games, the player's card or cards that are face down are referred to as "hole cards", as in "To have an Ace in the hole".

Hole carding – Obtaining knowledge of cards that are supposed to be hidden from view, usually from a weak dealer or some form of cheating, thus gaining an unfair advantage in a game.

Hop bet – In a craps game, a bet that is determined on the next roll of the dice. This is a type of single roll proposition bet.

Hooch – Slang for alcoholic beverages.

Hopper – In slots, the internal container that holds the coins that are immediately available for payouts.

Horn bet – In a crap game, a one roll proposition bet on the 2, 3, 11, & 12. The bet is actually four separate bets, and pays off depending on which number is actually rolled, minus three units for the other three losing bets.

Horn High Bet – In craps, a bet on three of the horn numbers, with two units on the "high" number, using an entire $5 chip. (For example, you could place $1 each on 2, 3, 12, and $2 on the 11 – in this case, 11 is the high number, and is a "horn hi yo").

Host – A casino employee who takes care of needs for a high value player, such as making meal and room reservations, and administering comps to the player.

Hot – A player on a winning streak, or a slot machine that is playing out, is said to be hot.

House – Another name for the casino.

House Edge – (house advantage) - The house edge is the percentage of each bet you make that the casino takes in or retains. In order to get this edge, the winning wagers are paid out at less than true odd. It is regarded as the price you pay to play, or as an entertainment tax. Also known as the edge, the house advantage or HA.

House rules – The rules played in a particular venue not necessarily in alignment with normal or official rules.

House ways – In pai gow poker, the casino rules for setting the banker's hand.

Hustler – Slang for a person who knows how to get money or services from others.

IGT – International Game Technology Company

IMHO – In My Humble Opinion

Independent events (or trials) – Two events are independent if the results of one event do not affect the results of another subsequent event. For example when playing craps, throwing an 11 does not affect the probability that the next throw will or will not be an 11 (the dice do not have a memory). Likewise, with an unbiased roulette wheel, when the ball lands on a particular number, it does not have any affect the next spin, as the ball is just as likely to land on the same number again as it is to land on any other number. This is also referred to as independent trials.

Indian casino – Casino operation on an Indian reservation or other tribal land in the United States. Because these areas have tribal sovereignty, states have limited ability to forbid gambling there, as codified by the Indian Gaming Regulatory Act of 1988.

Inside bet – In craps, a bet on the four inside numbers; 5-6-8-9. See also "outside bet".

Inside bet – In roulette, a bet placed on one of the numbers, as opposed to on Red or Black, Dozens, or Even or Odd.

Insurance – In blackjack, a side bet called insurance is offered when the dealer's up card is an Ace. If the dealer has a natural 21 (an Ace & a 10 value card), then the insurance wager is paid off at 2:1, or double your original wager.

IRS Publication 17 – Your Federal Income Tax

IRS Publication 525 – Taxable and Nontaxable Income

IRS Publication 529 – Miscellaneous Deductions

Jackpot – The big win on a slot machine, as opposed to all of the little wins.

Juice – A person who knows all of the right people in a town is said to have the "juice", especially if the person is well connected in the casino, thus wielding a lot of power. Also a slang term for interest or vigorish, as in "the juice is running".

Junket – A trip arranged by a casino for a group of players.

Kelly criterion – A mathematical formula used to determine the optimal size of a series of bets, based on a percentage of your edge.

Keno runner – The casino employee who takes your bet to the counter, and who will hopefully also deliver the payment for a winning ticket.

Kibitzer – A spectator at any game who looks at a player's hands and offers unwanted comments or advice.

Kicker – In cards, an unpaired high card held with one or more pairs, often used to determine the winning hand.

La bouchere – also called the cancellation system or split martingale, is a betting/gambling strategy used in roulette.

Ladder man – In baccarat, the supervisor who watches the game from a tall chair.

La partage – In roulette, with a single 0 (European wheel) when you make an even money (only) bet and you lose because the ball landed on 0, you immediately get half of your initial wager back. This is a mostly unknown rule that is very player friendly, and effectively cuts the house advantage in half, from 2.70% to 1.35%. See also "En prison".

Lady luck – The goddess of good fortune who occasionally smiles on the player.

Ladies bet – (Field bet) - In a crap game, slang for a wager that one of the numbers 2, 3, 4, 9, 10, 11, or 12 (in the field area of the layout) will appear on the next roll of the dice, and is also known as a "field bet".

Lamer – In craps, the small circular tokens used to display to the overhead security cameras certain situations that are occurring, such as a buy bet being placed, or a bet being turned on or off. In roulette, they are used to designate the value of the chips in play. In baccarat, they are used to keep track of the commission owed by a player.

Late betting – Is making a bet after the time when no more bets are to be taken. It is considered cheating because information may have become available (including the outcome of the event) that was not available to those making earlier bets. This is also called "past posting".

Late surrender – In blackjack, a rule allowing a player to forfeit 50% of the bet after the dealer has checked for a blackjack, and is a player friendly rule.

Law of Large Numbers (LLN) – The law in probability theory that describes the result of performing the same experiment a large number of times. According to the law, the average of the results obtained from a large number of trials should be close to the expected value, and will tend to become closer as more trials are performed. The LLN is important because it "guarantees" stable long-term results for random events. For example, while a casino may lose money in a single spin of the roulette wheel, its earnings will tend towards a predictable percentage over a large number of spins.

Lay bet – A lay bet is the opposite of a buy bet, where a player bets on a 7 to roll before the number that is laid. Just like the buy bet lay bets pay true odds, but because the lay bet is the opposite of the buy bet, the payout is reversed.

Laying odds – In a sports book, when you place a wager on the favorite in the contest, you must bet a little more in order to win a little less, and this is called laying or giving odds. Also when playing craps, a dark side player who is betting against the shooter can back up his original wager with an odds bet, and this is also called giving or laying odds. See "giving odds" and "taking odds".

Le grand natural – In baccarat, a two card total of 9, which is the best possible hand.

Le petit natural – In baccarat, a two card total of 8, and is the second best possible hand.

Leader board – In tournaments, a scoreboard that tells the relative position of players to the other contestants at any particular time.

Left pocket money – From the practice of keeping your bankroll in one pocket and your spending money in another pocket.

Lid – On a gaming table, the clear acrylic box that covers the chips when the game is closed.

Line – In most sporting events, both sides are not usually equal in talent or ability. The line (or the spread) is the sports book's method of measuring this inequality, in order to allow for fair wagers on both sides of the event. An oddsmaker sets or develops the line. See also "point spread".

Line bet – In craps, a bet on either the pass or don't pass line.

Line bet – In roulette, a six number bet, placed on the outside line at the intersection of two rows.

Linemaker – The person who sets the odds and point spreads, and is also called the odds-maker.

Little Joe – In craps, a common name (slang) for the hard 4, shown as 2-2 on the dice.

Loaded dice – Dice that are weighted so that, no matter which way they are thrown, the weight in them causes them to flip with a predetermined number on top.

Load up – To play the maximum number of coins in a slot machine.

Loaded pull – Slang for playing a slot machine with maximum amount of coins.

Loader – A weak dealer who carelessly flashes the hole card when dealing.

Lock – A hand that cannot lose.

Lock it up – Dealer term to put loose chips into their stacks or into the house bank.

Long con – A confidence game that has many parts and players, often taking a considerable time (days or weeks) to complete. See also "short con".

Long shot – The player, horse, or team that is unlikely to win.

Loose (slots) – A slot machine that pays off very liberally (or frequently).

Loss – Much, much worse than a win.

Low hand – In pai gow poker, the two card hand placed closest to the dealer, also called the front hand. Can also be called the small, top, hair, or minor hand.

Luck – A temporary deviation or fluctuation from the expected norm, and the only way to explain someone else's good fortune, as in "she is SO lucky'.

Luminous reader – A cheating device used to view marked cards, usually in the form of glasses or a visor. See also "daub".

Mark – Slang for the potential victim of a con, the sucker. Can also be the sheep, fish, pigeon, or sucker.

Marked cards – Playing cards that are printed or altered so that the cheater can know the value of specific cards while only looking at the back of the card.

Marker – A player who has pre-established credit at a casino can "ask for" or "take out" a marker at the table. This is for all practical purposes a "check" that is cashed at the table to provide chips to play. See also "credit limit".

Martingale – A classic betting style, where gamblers increase bets after each loss in hopes that an eventual win will recover all previous losses.

Match play coupon – Free playing money (to bet with) found in coupon books given out by some casinos.

Mechanic – Slang name of a person who cheats, usually by manipulating playing cards.

Mid shoe entry – In blackjack, entering the game while in progress as opposed to at the beginning of a new deck.

Money line – This is the betting line that is offered by some sports books. See the "line".

Money plays – On table games, playing with actually cash instead of chips. Wagers made with cash are paid with chips.

Monster Roll – In craps, a "hot roll" lasting more than 20 minutes or that generates a lot of winnings for the players.

Mop – In craps, slang for the stick used by the stickperson to move the dice. See also "whip".

Muck – In card games, the pile of discards is called the muck, or the action of throwing in your hand (mucking). Hand mucking may also refer to a form of sleight of hand where a player conceals a card in his hand, and if used in a card game, is one type of cheating.

Natural – In blackjack, a natural is a 2 card hand that contains an Ace and a ten value card, for a total of 21 (also referred to as a blackjack). In baccarat, a 2 card total of 8 is a "le petit natural" and a 2 card total of a 9 is a "le grand natural". In craps, a come out roll of a 7 or 11 is a winner, and called a natural.

Near miss – In slots, is a reference to the small amount or win paid out often to keep a player seated and continuously betting, and is also sometimes called a taste.

Necktying – An action by a hand held card dealer where the front of the deck is predominately displayed instead of the top of the deck, to hide or camouflage the dealing of the second card as a form of cheating.

Neighbors – In roulette, the numbers adjacent to the winning number, on the left and right.

Nickels – $5 red chips are called "nickels", and helps to devalue them in the players mind.

Nina – Slang for a nine.

Number pool – The number pool is the range of numbers from which you may select the numbers you wish to play. Most lottery pools have a range of 1 to 60, while most keno ranges are 1 to 80.

Numbers – Slang for the point spread.

Nuts (the nuts) – In poker, the nut hand, is the strongest possible hand in a given situation.

Odds – The odds tells you how many times something *will not* happen in relation to how many times it *will* happen, and is expressed as 6 to 1 (or 6:1 or 6/1)) for the example of the odds that today is Friday, because in a normal week, there are 6 ways for it not to be Friday and 1 way for it to be Friday.

Odds bet – In craps, after a point is established or a come bet has traveled to a number, additional money can be wagered along with the original bet, and this additional money has no house advantage on it.

Oddsmaker – The person who sets the odds and point spreads, and is also called the line-maker.

Oddsman bet – In craps, a player can sometimes (varies by casino) make an free odds bet for themselves for the unused amount of another player's pass line odds bet if that player is not using the total (or maximum) odds bet allowed. See also "taking odds".

Off – In craps, a player may "turn off" some wagers without actually removing them from the table layout, by simply telling the dealer "I am off on so & so" or "Turn off my so & so". The dealer acknowledges this and places a small button on your bet that says OFF, so the security camera can record this transaction. These bets are temporarily no longer at risk. When ready, the player tells the dealer to "Turn me back on" and the button is removed. See also "working" and "on", as well as "down".

On – In craps, a player may "turn on" certain bets that may not normally be active, by simply telling the dealer to "Work my so & so". The dealer acknowledges this and places a small button on your bet that says ON, so the security camera can record this transaction. These bets will normally become active on their own at some point during the roll, and the button will then be removed. See also "working" and "off".

One armed bandit – Common slang name of a slot machine, from the single arm that was pulled in the past to activate the reels.

Open – In poker, to make the first bet.

Open stakes – The alternative to table stakes rules is called "open stakes", in which players are allowed to buy more chips during the hand and even to borrow money (often called "going light"). Open stakes are most commonly found in home or private games. In casinos, players are sometimes allowed to buy chips at the table during a hand, but are never allowed to borrow money or use IOUs. See "table stakes".

Opening line – The initial point spread released for a game.

Outs – Options, as in "I still have a few outs left".

Outside bet – In craps, a bet on the four outside numbers; 4-5-9-10. See also "inside bet".

Outside bet – In roulette, a bet placed on other than the inside numbers, such as even money bets, column bets, and dozens bets.

Orange chips – $1000 chips are usually orange in color. See also "Pumpkin".

Over – The "over" is a sports bet that the combined final total score of both teams will be over a specific total. See also "the under".

Overlay – An overlay is a bet where you have an edge over the casino.

Outcome – One possible specific result of a trial, such as two dice landing on the 5 & 6 for an outcome of 11. This is different than an event.

Ozzie and Harriet – In crap, slang for a hard 8 (two 4s), as they were considered squares. See also "square pair".

Pack – In blackjack, the full amount of cards (all decks) in play at the table.

Paddle – The plastic device that dealers use to push money into the drop box.

Paint – Another name for a face card or a picture card, such as a jack, queen, or a king.

Palm – Method of hiding a card in the hand for the purpose of switching it or stealing it as a form of cheating.

Pari-mutuel betting – Is a betting system in which all bets of a particular type are placed together in a pool; taxes and a house "take" or "vig" are removed, and payoff odds are calculated by sharing the pool among all winning bets. Pari-mutuel betting differs from fixed-odds betting in that the final payout is not determined until the pool is closed – in fixed odds betting, the payout is agreed at the time the bet is sold. Pari-mutuel gambling is frequently state-regulated, and offered in many places where gambling is otherwise illegal, and is often offered at "off track" facilities, where players may bet on the events without actually being present to observe them in person.

Parlay – In sports betting, a "parlay" is a wager with 2 or more outcomes tied together, and all must win in order for the parlay wager to win. In gaming, to "parlay" is to increase your bet by the amount you just won. In other words you are leaving your entire win on the table with the original bet as a new, much larger wager.

Past posting – Is making a bet after the time when no more bets are to be taken. It is considered cheating because information may have become available (including the outcome of the event) that was not available to those making earlier bets. This is also called "late betting".

Pat hand – In blackjack, a "pat hand" is an unbusted hand worth as least 17, and you do not wish to add another card to it, you are said to be "Standing pat". See also "stiff hand".

Pay cycle – A pay cycle is a theoretical expression that reflects the number of plays required for the machine to cycle through all of the winning and non-winning combinations. As payouts are randomized, a machine will not hit each possible combination exactly once during each complete pay cycle.

Pay line – The pay line is the line across a slot machine display on which the symbols must line up. Some machines have only 1 pay line, while other may have 25 or more, requiring many more coins per spin.

Payoff – The payoff (or payback) is the return you receive on a wager.

Payout percentage – The payout percentage (or payback %) is the preprogrammed percent of each dollar wagered that a slot machine returns to the player. Payback percentage is 100% minus the house edge.

Payout table – The payout table (or schedule) is posted on a video poker machine (or its display) that tells you what each winning hand will pay for the number of coins or credits wagered.

Peeker (or Peeper) – On a blackjack table, the small mirror device the dealer uses to check his hole card.

Peeking – A cheating method to secretly see the value of a card.

Penetration – In blackjack, the percentage of cards dealt prior to a shuffle, with deeper penetration being more player friendly.

Penny ante – A small stakes game.

Penny chips – Slang for white $1 chips, which are sometimes referred to as "penny chips". See also "whites".

Picture card – Another name for a face card such as a jack, queen, or a king.

Pigeon – Slang for the mark or sucker in a con. Also the "fish" or "sheep".

Pill – In roulette, a slang name for the ball.

Pinch – To remove chips from a losing bet (opposite of capping) and is a form of cheating.

Pip – The spot on a die.

Pit – An area of the casino floor where table games are located, which are usually arranged in some sort of an oval. Dealers, supervisors, and bosses stand on the inside of the pit, and the players stand or sit along the outside edges of the tables.

Pit boss – The pit boss is the person who supervises all of the games and casino personnel in a particular pit area for that shift.

Pivot point – With card counting, the point in the count when it becomes positive or negative.

Place – In craps, to "place" a number is to make a wager on a particular point (or points); betting that this number will be rolled before the 7 is rolled.

Player card – A card (also called a slot card) issued by the casino which is used by the player to accumulate points towards comps, and is also used as a marketing tool by the casino.

Player hand – In baccarat, the first of the two hands dealt.

Ploppy – Derogatory slang term for clueless players who have no idea what they are doing.

Pocket – In roulette, the individual numbered areas on the wheel where the balls lands are called the "pockets", and typically alternate between red and black in color.

Point – In craps, the point numbers are the 4, 5, 6, 8, 9, & 10.

Point box – In craps, one of the six numbered boxed above the come line where individual bets are placed by the dealer.

Point spread – The point spread (the line) is quoted by the sports books to equalize the attractiveness of betting on each team. The outcome of a point spread wager is determined by adjusting the final score by the numbers of points in the spread. See also "line".

Poke – Rarely used slang term for a bankroll.

Poker – A card game with many variations, where the player usually play against each other and not the house.

Post – To place a bet.

Pot – The pot is the pile of chips that accumulates in a card game as each player antes, bets, and raises. The pot goes to the winner of the hand.

Preferential shuffling – In blackjack, a technique used to foil card counters which involves reshuffling early (before reaching the cut card) when the count is favorable to the players, but continuing to deal without shuffling when the count is unfavorable to the player.

Pressing – Similar to a parlay, a "pressed" bet leaves a portion of the win on the table with the original bet, creating a new larger wager. While a parlay leaves 100% of the win on the table, a press bet leaves less than 100% of the win on the table and takes a portion of the win off of the table as profit.

Probability – Probability is the way of expressing mathematical knowledge or belief that a particular event will happen, and is used extensively in gambling to draw conclusions (or infer) about the likelihood of the occurrence of potential events, ranging from the impossible (0) to the certain (1). From the Latin probabilis which means "resembling truth".

Progressive – A progressive is a slot machine whose jackpot keeps increasing each time a coin is played.

Progressive slots – A group of slot machines that are linked together and which pool a fraction of each wager into a very large jackpot.

Proposition bet – a bet made regarding the occurrence or non-occurrence of an event during a game not directly affecting the game's final outcome.

Puck – In craps, the puck is marker that is used to indicate that a point has been established, and is placed on that particular point at each end of the table. It has a white "ON" side and a black "OFF" side, and is about 3 inches in diameter. Also called a "Buck".

Pumpkins – Orange $1000 chips are often called "pumpkins".

Punto banco – Another name for Baccarat as played in North America.

Puppy paws – Slang in cards for the suit of Clubs. Also the informal name of the dice design of the number 5. See also "quincunx".

Purple chips – $500 chips are usually purple in color. See also "Barney".

Push – A push is a tie outcome between the dealer and the player, and no money changes hands. For example, in blackjack a "push" occurs when both the dealer and the player finish the hand with the same un-busted total.

Pushing the house – Attempting to get a better game from the casino than it advertises.

Put bet – In craps, is a pass line bet that is placed after the point is already established.

Quads – Slang for 4 of a kind in cards.

Quarters – $25 green chips are called "quarters", and helps to devalue them in the players mind.

Quincunx – On a die, the name of the pattern of the side with the number 5 on it. See also "puppy paw".

Rabbit hunting – Asking to see what cards would have come up if a hand had continued.

Racino – A combination pari-mutual venue (horse track, dog track or jai alai court) and a casino. Typically, a racino offers only slot machine games.

Rack – A plastic tray used to store and transport coins, chips, or tokens.

Rail – The rail is the inside edge of a racetrack, the spectator gallery in a poker room, or the physical top edge of a crap table.

Rail birds – People who attempt to steal other player's chips off of the rail in a crap game.

Rake – The rake is the money the casino or card room charges for each hand of a card game.

Random – Unpredictable, and implies that results of a set of outcomes can, may or will be different even if the influences appear to be identical.

Randomness – The concept of non-order or non-coherence in a sequence of numbers (or steps or symbols) such that there is no intelligible pattern or combination that can be predetermined.

Random number generator (RNG) – The computer chip in slot machines that generate a sequence of numbers or symbols that lack any pattern.

Rank – In cards, the numerical value.

Rat hole – Hiding or removing some of your chips (into a pocket or purse) off of a table game to give the appearance to the dealer of having lost more than you actually have is referred to as "rat holing" chips, and is considered to be bad form. Also called "going south".

Rat pack – A group of actors originally centered on Humphrey Bogart. In the mid-1960s it was the name used by the press and the general public to refer to a later variation of the group (after Bogart's death) that called itself "the summit" or "the clan," featuring Frank Sinatra, Dean Martin, Sammy Davis, Jr., Peter Lawford, and Joey Bishop.

Rating – The casino rating (or ranking) of players based on how much and for how long they gamble, which is then used to determine what comps may be given out.

Readers – Slang for a marked deck of cards.

Red chips – $5 chips are usually red in color, and are often called "nickels" or "reds".

Reel – A spinning wheel inside a slot machine window on which the various symbols are printed. In the newer video displays, the reels are virtual.

Represent – In cards, to play as if holding a certain hand, as in "he is representing aces".

RFB – The big comp of Room, Food, & Beverages. See also "RLF".

RFID tags – Radio Frequency Identification tags are often installed in higher value chips, and allow casinos the ability to detect counterfeit chips, track betting habits of individual players, speed up chip tallies, and determine counting mistakes of dealers.

Rich deck – In blackjack, is a deck whose remaining cards are favorable to the player.

Right bettor – In craps, a right bettor is betting that the pass line and come bets will win; as opposed to a "wrong bettor" (dark side player) who is betting that the pass line and come bets will lose. Both are correct ways to play.

Riffle test – A method of checking a card deck for hidden markings.

Risk – A state of uncertainty where some of the possibilities involve loss or other undesirable outcomes.

Risk of ruin – The probability of losing a bankroll to the point at which continued playing is no longer a valid option.

River – In cards, the fifth and final community card.

River bet – On some roulette layouts (especially in "riverboat" casinos near major rivers) there may be a "meandering" line across the columns and rows covering 12 numbers (the same as a column) which is referred to as the "river bet".

Riverboat Casino – A casino built on a boat or a barge, and that is on or very near a body of water, such as a lake or a river. Many casinos in the Midwest are this type because of state laws.

RLF – A smaller comp of a Room and Limited Food. See also "RFB".

Roll – In craps, to roll is to throw the dice. A legal roll requires both dice to hit and rebound off of the far wall, ensuring to the casino that the resultant number is random.

Roll up – Name for the noises and lights that accentuate a player's win on a slot machine.

Roulette – Is a casino game named after a French diminutive for *little wheel*. In the game, players may choose to place bets on either a single number or a range of numbers, the colors red or black, or whether the number is odd or even. To determine the winning number and color, a croupier spins a wheel in one direction, and then spins a ball in the opposite direction around a tilted circular track running around the circumference of the wheel. The ball eventually loses momentum and falls on to the wheel and into one of 37 (in French/European roulette) or 38 (in American roulette) colored and numbered pockets on the wheel, which determines the win.

Roulette chips – These are casino issued chips for playing roulette only, and may not be used for any other games. For American roulette, there are specific sets of plain chips with no value printed on them in 6 to 10 different colors, with a single color given to each player so that their chips can be easily identifiable on the table. See also "wheel checks".

Round – In card games, a round could either mean a round of hands, or a round of betting within a round of hands.

Rounder – A person who makes a significant portion of their income from playing poker, often travelling around from city to city seeking high stakes cash games. See also "grinder".

Rule card – In baccarat, the card that shows the rules for play.

Rush – Being extremely lucky and winning a large proportion of bets is said to be "on a rush."

S17 – In blackjack, the rule where a dealer must stand on a soft 17. This is a player friendly rule. See also "H17".

SAR – Suspicious Activity Report - is a report made by a financial institution or casino to the Financial Crimes Enforcement Network (FinCEN), regarding suspicious or potentially suspicious monetary activity. The primary use is to combat money laundering and fraud.

Sacred money – (scared money) - Any portion of your gambling bankroll that you are afraid to lose or can't afford to lose, such as the grocery or rent money.

Sandbag – To play deceptively in order to draw others into a bet. An example might be betting very low when you have a very good hand, in order to entice others to play along in order to build the pot. See also "slow play", "check raise" and "stall".

Sawdust joint – Slang for an unpretentious casino.
Scared money – (sacred money) – Any portion of your gambling bankroll that you are afraid to lose or can't afford to lose, such as the grocery or rent money.

Score – A win.

See – In poker, to match another player's bet. See also "call".

Sequence bets – In craps, sequence bets are wagers that require multiple rolls of the dice to reach a decision, as opposed to one-roll wagers that may be decided on the very next roll of the dice. The pass and come bets are sequence bets.

Session – A series of plays over a period of time are "sessions". An example would be to play for a 2 hour session in the morning, and then another after dinner.

Set – A pai gow poker player "sets" their 7 cards into a 2 card hand and a 5 card hand. Also, three of a kind in poker.

Setting the dice – In craps, the practice of arraigning the dice in a particular order prior to throwing them.

Seven out – At craps, when a point is established and then a 7 rolls, the player has "sevened out", and that hand ends and the dice are passed to the next player.

Shark – Slang for a particularly treacherous or devious professional gambler and is a very skilled player; also in today's usage can mean swindler or villain.

Sharp – (Sharper) – One who cheats or swindles.

Sheep – Slang for the mark or sucker in a con. Also known as a "fish" or "pigeon".

Shill – A casino employee who acts as a customer (or player) at an empty table to attract other players to begin to gamble at that table. Also, any additional players in a confidence game or con.

Shiner – A small hidden mirror used by a dealer to see every card dealt, and is a form of cheating. Also called a "twinkle".

Shoe – A plastic or wooded tray or box that holds three or more decks of cards. 1 & 2 deck games are usually hand held and dealt (pitch games), while games with 3-6 or more decks are usually dealt from a shoe.

Shoes – In craps, slang for when there is a pass line bet for the dealers, and it is backed up with odds, the bet is said to "have shoes".

Shooter – In craps, the player rolling (or throwing) the dice is "the shooter", and the fate of the entire table is in his hands.

Short con – A simple confidence game that has an almost immediate outcome, as opposed to the "long con".

Short deck – A card deck with a few key cards removed to gain an unfair advantage over another player or players.

Short odds – Less than true odds.

Short pay – In slots, a type of machine that pays less than the best (full pay) machine in the same variation.

Shuffling – A procedure used to randomize a deck of playing cards to provide an element of chance in card games. Shuffling is often followed by a cut, to help ensure that the shuffler has not manipulated the outcome.

Shutter – On a reusable bingo card, the "shutter" is the small plastic piece that slides over the number to mark it as having been called.

Side bet – Many table games may offer another bet, called the side bet, in addition to the main or primary bet. An example of this is the "insurance bet" in blackjack.

Sin City – A slang name today for Las Vegas, and other major cities in the past.

Skill stop – A slot machine that lets players stop reels individually, thereby letting them use skill (in theory) to increase their chances of lining up a paying combination.

Skinny – In craps, slang for a bet on Any Seven. See also "Big Red".

Slot card – Another name for the player card issued by the casino.

Slot club – Program in place at most casinos which provide comps to slot players.

Slot handle – The amount of money placed in a slot machine over a period of time.

Slot hold percentage – The percentage of the slot handle won or retained by the casino.

Slow play – To play deceptively in order to draw others into a bet. An example might be betting very low when you have a very good hand, in order to entice others to play along in order to build the pot. See also "sandbag" and "stall".

Slug – Fake coin used in older slot machines. Also the name for the group of cards between the cut cards in shoe dealt games.

Snake eyes – In craps, when a 2 is rolled (two 1s) it is often called "snake eyes" (slang).

Snapper – Slang for a natural in blackjack.

Soft count – The activity in which soft money (paper currency, checks, & markers) are counted, in a special room under tight security.

Soft hand – In blackjack, any hand that contains an Ace counted as 11 is a soft hand. An example would be an Ace and a 7, for a soft 18. A soft hand may receive another hit card without fear of busting.

Spades – The highest value of the 4 suits in a deck of cards – Clubs, Diamonds, Hearts, then Spades. To have something in abundance is referred to as "in spades".

Spadille – Slang for the Ace of Spades. Also the name of the highest trump card in some card games.

Split – In blackjack, to divide a pair into two separate hands by placing an addition wager similar to the original.

Split bet – In roulette, is a bet that is placed on the line between two adjacent numbers, in effect betting half on each number. This will give the player two chances to win with a single bet, but only pays half as much.

Spread, bet – In blackjack, the amount that you vary your bet depending on the favorably of the count, in units. An example would be spreading your bets from $5 to $25 (1 unit to 5 units) when the count goes positive.

Spread, point – The point spread (the line) is quoted by the sports books to equalize the attractiveness of betting on each team. The outcome of a point spread wager is determined by adjusting the final score by the numbers of points in the spread. See also "line".

Sports book – A facility inside the casino (usually) that accepts wagers on sporting events is called a sports book.

Spot – A spot is one of the numbers that a player marks on a keno ticket. It also refers to the type of keno ticket played, such as a "6-spot" or a "10-spot" ticket. In table games, a "spot" refers to one of the player positions (as in "Is this spot taken?"), and on a treasure map, X always marks the spot.

Square pair – In craps, slang for a hard 8 (two 4s). See also "Ozzie & Harriet".

Stacked deck – A card deck that has been arranged to give someone the advantage, and is no longer random. This is sometimes used in the phrase, "He was playing against a stacked deck".

Stake – Another term for the bankroll you will use in a gambling session.

Stake horse – A person who provides a stake or bankroll to another person as an investment for a percentage of the win. As in, "My partner is stake horsing me for 25%".

Stall – To play deceptively in order to draw others into a bet. An example might be betting very low when you have a very good hand, in order to entice others to play along in order to build the pot. See also "slow play" and "sandbag".

Stand (Stand pat) – In blackjack, to "stand" is to decline to receive a hit card (stopping – or standing – with the total you have).

Steaming – Slang for when a player is "on tilt".

Street bet – In roulette, a bet places on a set of three numbers.

Street craps – Craps game played somewhere other than on a crap table, with betting limited to the come out roll and the point only. Players cover each other's bets, with no bank involved.

Stick – In craps, the wooden device use to move the dice around the table. See also "mop". Also slang for a shortened version of "stickman".

Stickman – In craps, the person who moves the dice around and calls out the numbers rolled is the "stickman", no matter the sex of the person working the stick.

Stiff – A gambler who does not tip is referred to as a "stiff".

Stiff hand – In blackjack, a "stiff hand" is a hand that is not pat, and may bust with a hit card, such as a hard 12-16. See also "pat hand".

Sting – The moment where a con artist takes the victim's money.

Stop-loss – is setting a limit on how much you will allow yourself to lose (when it's not going your way) before you stop playing, so you don't lose your entire bankroll in one session.

Stops – In slots, the reel's symbols and blank spaces that can line up on a pay line.

Straight up bet – In roulette, a bet on a single number, which if won, pays 35 to 1.

Street bet – In roulette, a bet on the 3 numbers across the columns.

Structuring – Arranging cash outs and/or deposits to avoid triggering reporting limits, and is considered to be illegal.

Sucker – The victim or "mark" in a con.

Sucker bet – A bet that you cannot win, or a bet that pays off at a very reduced rate. Also a bet or wager that is designed to lure you into a con.

Sucker's bet – In roulette, on an American Roulette table, the bet that covers 0, 00, 1, 2 and 3 has the worst odds of any bet in roulette, and is therefore called the Sucker's Bet.

Suit – A slang term for the supervisors who gather around in the pit to watch a player. Also any one of the 4 suits of cards; such as clubs, diamonds, hearts, & spades.

Sure thing – A guaranteed winner.

Surrender – In blackjack, to "surrender" is to give up half of your wager for the privilege of not playing out a poor hand (this option is not offered everywhere). See "early surrender" and "late surrender". A player friendly rule.

Surrender – In roulette, surrender means you only lose (in effect) half of your even-money bets when the ball lands on 0 or 00 (again this is not offered everywhere). A player friendly rule.

Sweating the money – When casino employees hover over the game, checking the payouts and worrying about loses, they are said to be "sweating the money", as if it comes out of their own pockets. See also "heat".

Symbols – The pictures on the reels of a slot machine, such as cherries, bells or $ signs.

System – A method of wagering a player may use to attempt to gain an advantage over the casino. The casinos love systems players, and will usually send the private jet to pick them up, which should tell you that systems do not work.

Table layout – The colorful markings on the table surface that tell the player where to place bets.

Table limit – Is the minimum and maximum bet that a gambler can make at a gaming table. Normally, these limits are set to optimize the return from the available seats. Since all table games give the house an advantage, the larger the bets, the larger the house's profit. So the house needs to manage the minimum bets to keep the seats full. This usually results in a low limit early in the day when there are fewer players with the table limits increasing as more players become available.

Table stakes – The buy in or stake that a player places on the table at the beginning of a game, and may not be changed or increased once a game begins. See also "open stakes".

Take a shot – To go for it, as in "I took a shot and lost everything".

Take down – In craps, to remove a bet from the table prior to the next roll of the dice.

Taking odds – A sports bettor "takes odds" when betting on the underdog by betting a lesser amount to win greater amount.

Taking odds – In craps, after a point is established and you have a pass line wager or a come bet that has traveled to a number, you can place additional money into the game that the house has no advantage on (no-vig or HA) by "taking odds". See also "giving odds" or "laying odds".

Taking care of the boys – Slang for tipping the dealers, regardless of sex.

Talisman – As a superstition, can be any small object but its most important characteristic is its alleged power to protect its owner from danger or harm, or to bring good luck. See also "amulet".

Tapped out – To lose all of your bankroll is said to be tapped or tapped out. Also, the phrase used when you are asked by the casino not to play any longer at a specific game, as in "I was tapped out of blackjack because my game was too strong for them". This comes from being tapped on the shoulder by a casino employee, asking you not to play.

Taste – In slots, is a reference to the small amounts or wins paid out often to keep a player seated and continuously betting, and is also sometimes called a near miss.

Tax avoidance – Encouraged, and is the legal utilization of the tax regime to one's own advantage to reduce the amount of tax that is payable by means that are within the law.

Tax evasion – Illegal, and usually entails taxpayers deliberately misrepresenting or concealing the true state of their affairs to the tax authorities to reduce their tax liability and includes in particular dishonest tax reporting, such as declaring less income, profits or gains than actually earned or overstating deductions.

Taxes – A slang term for the House Advantage. See also "Vig" and "Juice".

Tell – A tell in poker is a detectable change in a player's behavior or demeanor that gives clues to that player's assessment of his hand. A player gains an advantage if he observes and understands the meaning of another player's tell, particularly if the tell is unconscious and reliable.

Theoretical ("thoe" for short) – is the amount of money a player is expected to lose based on the long run statistical advantage the casino has on the particular game being played.

Third base – In blackjack, the position nearest the dealer's right is "third base" and will be dealt to and played last, and is sometimes referred to as the anchor position. See also "first base" and "anchor position".

Three Card Monti – An old swindle in which the operator tosses three cards onto the table, usually played on the street. One of these cards is the "money card" and the players are supposed to guess which one it is. Due to sleight of hand or outright cheating, winning this con is not possible, although it always appears to be very easy to beat. There are numerous other names for this game, such as: Three-card shuffle, Menage-a-card, Triplets, Follow the lady, *Les Trois Perdants* (French for Three Losers), *le Bonneteau*, Find the lady, *Bola bola* or Follow the Bee. In its full form, Three-card Monte is an example of a classic "short con" in which a shill pretends to conspire with the mark to cheat the dealer, while in fact conspiring with the dealer to cheat the mark.

Tidy the Bowl – In craps, the stickperson keeping (or putting) the extra dice in a neat row, or in the provided bowl.

Tier score / level – For player cards, your Tier Score is a running total of Tier Credits you have earned for the year, and determines your Tier level.

Tilt or "On tilt" – Is poker jargon for letting frustration or other emotional stress interfere with one's poker-playing judgment, and can apply to any game. A state of emotional upset, mental confusion or frustration in which a player adopts a less than optimal strategy, usually resulting in poor play and poor performance.

Time and a half – Slang for the blackjack payout of 3:2 for a natural.

TITO – Ticket-In / Ticket-Out is now used in many casino slot machines to print out a slip of paper with a barcode indicating the amount of money represented. These can in turn be redeemed for cash at an automated kiosk.

Toke – Another name for a dealer tip or gratuity. "To toke" is to give a tip for a service.

Toke board – In a sports book, a chart that posts races, teams, contests, and either the odds or the line.

Toke box – Serves as a repository for cash and chips given to the dealer as tokes (tips).

Toke hustling – Dealers who ask for tokes and/or for bets to wagered for them are referred to as toke hustlers, and this practice is usually discouraged by US casinos.

Tom – Slang for no good or not generous with tips, and is the opposite of a "George".

Total – The total is the combined scores of both teams, which can be wagered on in a sports book. You can also bet the "over" or the "under", in relation to the actual total or some other predetermined total.

Touch screen – A video slot or poker machine that can be touched by finger tip to select an object or option.

Tournament – A gaming competition.

Tout – To sell tips or information on upcoming contests.

Trespassed – Being escorted off of a casino property, with the threat of arrest for trespassing if you return.

Trips – In cards, slang for three of a kind.

True odds – This is the ratio (usually referred to as the odds) of the number of times that one event will occur to the number of times that another event will occur. A true odds payout means that there is no house advantage (HA) on the wager.

TTO – This Time Only, as a one-time extension of a player's credit line.

Tub – In craps, a small one or two dealer craps table used usually in small casinos, and is also called a "Mini" or "Half-Table".

Turning the Dice – In craps, when the stickperson flips the dice around with his stick in order to make sure a 7, 11, 2, 3, or 12 isn't showing when they go to the shooter.

Twenty one (21) – Another name for blackjack.

Twinkle – A small hidden mirror used by a dealer to see every card dealt, and is a form of cheating. Also called a "shiner".

Two way bet – Is a bet that is part for the player and part for the dealers.

Under – The "under" is a sports bet that the combined final total score of both teams will be under a specific total. See also "the over".

Underdog – The predicted loser in a sports event. See also "dog" and "favorite".

Underlay – An underlay is a bad bet, and an event that has more money wagered on its happening than can be justified by the true odds of the event happening.

Uniform distribution – A probability distribution in which every possible outcome is equally likely. For example, with an unbiased roulette wheel, every possible number is equally likely to be an outcome on any particular spin. However in craps, the numbers that come up are not at all uniform in distribution.

Unit – The size of a single bet used as a standard of measurement.

Up card – In blackjack, the dealer's card that is placed face up for everyone to see is referred to as the up card.

Value Bet – A bet you make, believing it will earn slightly more than it will lose over the long run, when the pot payout exceeds the odds of winning.

Variability – Short term deviations from the expected outcome.

Variance – The variance is a parameter that describes a theoretical probability of distribution of a set of outcomes, and is a measure of how far a set of numbers is spread out.

Vig – Short for Vigorish, and is also known as the juice or the take. It is typically referred to as the commission or fee paid to a service (bookkeeper) for providing the service (the sports book). The vig is a fee that is paid in addition to the actual wager, which is different than the HA, which is a fee that is deducted from winning wagers by paying less than true odds. In craps, certain wagers have a vig associated with them in order to make that particular wager.

VIP – A big bettor to the casino who receives full RFB treatment (and more) is considered a VIP, or Very Important Person.

Virtual casino – An online casino, which may allow gambling with real money.

Volatility – The short term fluctuations in payback.

W2-G – IRS form issued to the player for "Certain Gambling Winnings" – usually for amounts in excess of $1200, with a copy going to the IRS.

W-9 – IRS form "Request for Taxpayer Identification Number and Certification"

Waddler – People who take up the entire space in the isle by moving VERY slowly while looking at everything, usually when you are in a hurry.

Wager (or bet) – The act of placing a bet is called making a wager. Or as a bet, it is the amount of money that is risked on the outcome of an individual event.

Walking with the money – Leaving a casino with money from casino credit or a marker, is referred to as "walking with the money", and while not illegal is very bad form.

Wall (or back wall) – In craps, the end of the table the where shooter throws the dice against in order to complete a fair roll. As in "Please hit the back wall".

Wash – Where one bet cancels out another bet.

Washing the cards – When several new decks of cards are combined together, they are randomly spread out on the table surface, and then mixed together, in a process called "washing the cards" prior to being shuffling.

Way ticket – A way ticket is a keno ticket that groups different numbers together to create more than one way to win. Each group contains the same amount of numbers. See also "combination ticket".

Weight count – In slots, refers to the dollar amount of coins or tokens removed from a slot machine's drop bucket or drop box and counted by the casino's hard count team through the use of a weigh scale.

Whale – Another name for an extreme high roller, or a very large player (money wise).

Wheel – Slang for roulette.

Wheel Checks – Unique unmarked chips used specifically on roulette tables. See also "roulette chips".

Whip – In craps, the stick used by the stickperson to move the dice. See also "mop".

Whirl (or world) bet – In a craps game, is a five-unit bet that is a combination of a horn and any-seven bet, with the idea that if a seven is rolled the bet is a push, because the money won on the seven is lost on the horn portions of the bet.

White chips – $1 chips are usually white (or light blue) in color, and are often referred to as "whites". See also "penny chips".

White meat – After paying off a marker, any win left over is sometimes referred to as "the white meat".

Wild card – In cards, a joker or other designated card(s) that can be used as any other card to complete your hand.

Win – Much, much better than a loss.

Win/Loss statements – Tax documents from the casino.

Wonging – In blackjack, involves watching the play of cards in a game without actually wagering your own money, until the count becomes advantageous, and then stepping in and playing only while the count remains in the player's favor, and then stepping out again. "Wonging" is the reason that some casinos have signs on some blackjack tables saying, "No Mid-Shoe Entry," meaning that a new player must wait until exactly the first hand after a shuffle to begin playing. After Stanford Wong who made the technique famous. See also "back counting".

World (or whirl) bet – In a crap game, is a five-unit bet that is a combination of a horn and any-seven bet, with the idea that if a seven is rolled the bet is a push, because the money won on the seven is lost on the horn portions of the bet.

Working – In craps, when a bet or wager is working, it is at risk on the next roll of the dice. Wagers that are normally off can be made to be working by telling the dealer to "Work my so & so". The dealer acknowledges this and places a small button on your bet that says ON, so the security camera can record this transaction. Bets that have been "turned off" can be turned back on by telling the dealer that your bets "are now working". See also "off" and "on".

Wrong bettor – In craps, a wrong bettor (dark side player) is betting that the pass line and come bets will lose; as opposed to the "right bettor" who is betting that the pass line and come bets will win. Both are correct ways to play.

WSOP – World Series of Poker

Yo (Yo-leven) – In craps, when the dice role shows an 11, it is called a "YO" or "Yo-leven" because "Eleven" can sound similar to "Seven".

Zukes – Another name (slang) for tips or tokes.

21 – Another name for blackjack.

3:2 – In blackjack, the normal payout for a natural win. See also "6:5".

3-4-5 odds – In craps, refers to the ratio of free odds in relation to the base bet, in units. So if you have a pass line bet of $5 – and the point becomes 4 or 10 you could add $15 in odds; with the 5 or 9 you could add $20; and with the 6 or 8 you could add $25. This is the same for come bets.

3 Card Monti – An old swindle in which the operator tosses three cards onto the table, usually played on the street. One of these cards is the "money card" and the players are supposed to guess which one it is. Due to sleight of hand or outright cheating, win-

ning this con is not possible, although it always appears to be very easy to beat. There are numerous other names for this game, such as: Three-card shuffle, Menage-a-card, Triplets, Follow the lady, *Les Trois Perdants* (French for Three Losers), *le Bonneteau*, Find the lady, *Bola bola* or Follow the Bee. In its full form, Three-card Monte is an example of a classic "short con" in which a shill pretends to conspire with the mark to cheat the dealer, while in fact conspiring with the dealer to cheat the mark.

6:5 – In blackjack, a reduced payout for a natural win, any is a very bad rule for the player. See also "3:2".

86 – Slang for being banned from or kicked out of a casino. As in "I was eighty-sixed from the Stardust when I was younger."

419 – (Advance Fee Fraud). Promising a victim a large sum of money if they invest a small amount of money. Called a 419 because this is the US Criminal Code covering this type of fraud.

1099 MISC – IRS form issued to a player for "Miscellaneous Income" after a machine win, with a copy going to the IRS.

CHAPTER 12

Bibliography

"If you steal from one author, it's plagiarism – but if you steal from many, it's research." Wilson Mizner, American playwright

"The secret to creativity is in knowing how to hide your sources." Albert Einstein

Barboianu, Catalin (2008). Understanding and Calculating the Odds, Infarom Publishing, Breiningsville, PA.

Blackwood, Kevin (2006). Casino Gambling for Dummies, Wiley Publishing Inc, Hoboken, NJ.

Burton, Bill (2005). 1000 Best Casino Gambling Secrets, Sourcebooks, Naperville, Il.

Epstein, Richard A (2009). The Theory of Gambling and Statistical Logic, 2nd edition, Elsevier –Academic Press, Burlington, MA.

Ford, James Harrison (2004). How to Gamble at the Casinos Without Getting Plucked Like a Chicken, El Paso Norte Press, El Paso, TX.

Griffen, Peter A (1999). The Theory of Blackjack, Huntington Press, Las Vegas, NV.

Gonick, Larry & Smith, Waollcott (1993). The Cartoon Guide to Statistics, Harper Collins Publishing, New York, NY.

Haigh, John (2009). Taking Chances – Winning With Probability. Oxford University Press, New York, NY.

Nestor, Basil (1999). The Unofficial Guide to Casino Gambling, Wiley Publishing Inc, Hoboken, NJ.

Packel, Edward (2006). The Mathematics of Games and Gambling – 2nd Edition, The Mathematical Association of America, Washington, DC.

Renneisen, Robert (1996). How to be Treated Like a High Roller, Carol Publishing Group, New York, NY.

Rubin, Max (2001). Comp City, A Guide to Free Casino Vacations – 2nd Edition, Huntington Press, Las Vegas, NV.

Scoblete, Frank (2010). Beat Blackjack Now – The easiest way to get the edge. Triumph Books, Chicago, IL.

Scoblete, Frank and Dominator (2005). Golden Touch Dice Control Revolution, Research Services Unlimited, Greensboro, NC.

Scoblete, Frank (2006). Golden Touch Black Jack Revolution, Research Services Unlimited, Greensboro, NC.

Scoblete, Frank (2003). Casino Gambling – Play Like a Pro in 10 Minutes or Less, Bonus Books, Chicago, IL.

Scott, Jean (2005). The Frugal Gambler – 2nd Edition, Huntington Press, Las Vegas, NV.

Scott, Jean & Chien, Marissa (2007). Tax Help for Gamblers, Huntington Press, Las Vegas, NV.

Shackleford, Michael (2005). Gambling 102 – The Best Strategies for All Casino Games, Huntington Press, Las Vegas, NV.

Shook, Robert L (2003). Jackpot! – Harrah's Winning Secrets for Customer Loyalty, John Wiley & Sons Inc, Hoboken, NJ.

Silberstang, Edwin (1997). The Winner's Guide to Casino Gambling, Penguin Books USA, New York, NY.

Taleb, Nassim Nicholas (2007). Fooled by Randomness, Penguin Books, USA, New York, NY.

Tamburin, Henry (1998). Henry Tamburin on Casino Gambling - The Best of the Best, Research Services Unlimited, Greensboro, NC.

Tamburin, Henry (1994). Black Jack - Take the Money and Run, Research Services Unlimited, Greensboro, NC.

Thorp, Edward (1984). The Mathematics of Gambling, Gambling Times, Hollywood, CA.

Vancura, Olaf (1996). Smart Casino Gambling, Index Publishing Group, San Deigo, CA.

Weaver, Warren (1982). Lady Luck – The Theory of Probably, Dover Publications, New York, NY.

Wong, Stanford & Spector, Susan (2005). The Complete Idiot's Guide to Gambling Like a Pro, Penguin Group, New York, NY.

Websites:

www.billburton.com – Casino and gambling writer for About.com.

www.bjmath.com – A good Blackjack math and general Blackjack information site.

www.goldentouchcraps.com – Everything to know about Advantage Craps.

www.queenofcomps.com – Jean Scott's site on saving money and maximizing comps.

www.readybetgo.com – Excellent for general information about games and myth busting.

www.thewizardofodds.com – Excellent site for general game mathematics and odds.

www.urbino.net – A casino and gaming management site.

www.missouririck.com – Missouri Rick's website

Websites for Atlantic City:

www.atlanticcity.net – #1 source for everything AC.

Websites for Tunica:

www.tunicacasinos.com – A guide to all the Tunica Casinos and Hotels.

Websites for Las Vegas:

www.lasvegasadvisor.com – Anthony Curtis's site on saving money in Las Vegas.

www.lasvegas4newbies.com – Great information for first time Las Vegas visitors.

When there is a problem:

www.gamblersanonymous.org

Made in the USA
Charleston, SC
23 February 2017